WHEELS
WITHIN
WHEELS

WHEELS WITHIN WHEELS

A study of the road lobby

Mick Hamer

Routledge & Kegan Paul London and New York

First published in 1987 by
Routledge & Kegan Paul Ltd
11 New Fetter Lane, London EC4P 4EE

Phototypeset in Linotron Sabon, 10 on 12 pt
by Input Typesetting Ltd, London SW19 8DR
and printed in Great Britain
by T. J. Press (Padstow) Ltd
Padstow, Cornwall

British Library Cataloguing in Publication Data

Hamer, Mick
    Wheels within wheels: a study of the road
    lobby.—(Geography, environment and
    planning)
    1. Road construction—Government policy
    —Great Britain   2. Pressure groups—
    Great Britain
    I. Title   II. Series
    388.1'0941   HE363.G7

ISBN 0–7102–1007–8

Contents

Foreword

In January 1987, Antony Jay and Jonathan Lynn, authors of the television programme *Yes Minister*, received a special Award from the Freedom of Information Campaign for their unparalleled contribution to exposing the mechanisms of government and the cynicism of Whitehall secrecy. At the same time, Nigel Hawthorne and Paul Eddington, the much-loved stars of that programme, received OBEs from the Prime Minister, presumably for having kept her amused!

Confronted with the circumlocutory cunning of *Yes Minister*'s civil servants and the genial complacency of its politicians, one can't help but laugh along with Mrs Thatcher. Yet it's all a bit close to the bone, especially if the laughter serves to maintain certain cosy illusions about the nature of government, rather than to expose them.

Paramount amongst these illusions is the long-cherished notion that policy is conscientiously welded together by ministers having thoughtfully considered the opinions of all interested parties under the guidance of wise and impartial civil servants.

With less of the humour but all of the bite of *Yes Minister, Wheels Within Wheels* nails that particular illusion. It painstakingly charts the rise and rise of the road lobby, from its first tentative muscle flexing over the need to improve road surfaces at the turn of the century, through to its heyday in the 1960s and its still dominant role in shaping policy in Mrs Thatcher's Britain.

The constituent parts of this network of vested interests are carefully identified, their relative influence assessed, and their lines of communication into the Department of Transport laid bare. A freemasonry of road-lovers emerges, carefully nurtured over long expense-account lunches, reinforced by patronage and assiduously served by the likes of Joe Peeler, erstwhile head of the department's Freight Directorate and ardent advocate of more lorries and bigger lorries on more roads and better roads.

Though the road lobby is usually very keen to play down its influence, the testimony of several ministers as to the real extent of its power provides chilling confirmation of exactly what's going on behind the scenes. But one ends up with little sympathy for these ministers, whichever party they represent, for it is they who have failed to establish the kind of integrated transport policies which alone would limit the road lobby's influence.

The simple but regrettable fact is that this country has no coherent transport policy, and it is the road lobby that has most effectively and consistently exploited this policy vacuum. One administration after another has closed railways, undermined the financial base of public transport, provided huge, hidden subsidies through the company car system, kept road spending immune from any cuts, and authorised road construction schemes in isolation from the wider context of land use and transport planning. As a consequence, Britain's rail system is desperately under-funded in comparison with most other EEC countries. The growth in road freight, the lack of public support for the railways and the insatiable demand for new roads, have left our railways in a powerless state and highly vulnerable to the current ideological assault of Mrs Thatcher.

The effects of the present Government's clear preference for road construction and private, motorised transport have recently been magnified by the abolition of the Metropolitan Authorities. The loss of democratic control and accountability, of the city-wide integration of different forms of transport, and of incentives for promoting public transport, is a serious blow.

But *Wheels Within Wheels* also charts the emergence and growth of the anti-roads lobby and the increasing influence of today's environmental organisations. Despite the massive boost that the road lobby has received from Mrs Thatcher's government, despite the huge disparity in resources between organisations like the British Roads Federation on the one hand, and Friends of the Earth and Transport 2000 on the other, the short-sightedness and intellectual bankruptcy of prevailing policies are becoming obvious to an ever larger number of people.

It's too easy to forget that we are all cogs within the wheels of today's transport policies. *Wheels Within Wheels* will undoubtedly strengthen the determination of those working for a fully integrated transport policy for the United Kingdom. The influence of the road lobby has vitiated proper transport planning for decades and greatly damaged the interest of millions of people who depend on public transport services – so much so that not even Nigel Hawthorne and Paul Eddington could laugh off the cumulative impact of such powerful vested interests on the quality of our lives and our environment.

Friends of the Earth is one of the country's leading environmental pressure groups. Besides transport it runs major campaigns on energy, recycling, pollution, countryside and tropical rain forests. FoE is a part of UK 2000 and is affiliated to Friends of the Earth International, a worldwide federation of 30 FoE national bodies.

In England and Wales Friends of the Earth has 30,000 national supporters and 220 active local groups, campaigning on a wide variety of environmental causes. FoE has 25 full-time staff in its central office in London, while there is an entirely separate Friends of the Earth Scotland.

For full details of how to join FoE, contact the Membership Secretary at our London address.

Jonathon Porritt
February 1987

Acknowledgements

I would like to thank the following organisations for helping me to gain access to archives and files in their possession: the AA, for the archives in the central reference library, the Cyclists' Touring Club for its archives, the Greater London Council for its road building files, the London School of Economics for the Rees Jeffreys' papers, the Public Record Office and Transport 2000 (for allowing me to cart away its road lobby files).

The staff of these organisations were extremely helpful and I would particularly like to thank Alan Leng and Dave Wetzel for their efforts.

I would like to thank the same organisations for allowing me to quote from copyright material which is in their possession. The material from the Public Record Office appears by permission of the controller of HM Stationery Office.

My thanks also to the Central Office of Information, the Ford Motor Company, *The Guardian*, and Transport and Road Research Laboratory and the Weiner Institute for permission to reproduce photographs and illustrations which are their copyright.

I would also like to thank Albert Booth, John Horam and Roger Liddle for agreeing to be interviewed and helping me with their valuable recollections.

My friends willingly accepted the burdens I lumbered them with. Adrian Atkinson and Peter Kay provided invaluable information. John Adams, Kerry Hamilton, Susan Hoyle, Dick Jones, Nick Lester, Don Mathew and Fred Pearce all read parts of the draft. Peter Addis allowed me to plunder his photographic files. Mike Cross and Debbie MacKenzie went out to take pictures for for me. Mike Cross whiled away a day correcting my manuscript.

Friends of the Earth provided me a grant to research the book, without which it would never have been written.

Finally I would like to thank the large number of people in the road lobby and the Department of Transport who have provided me with help and information. Their only reward is anonymity.

Preface

More than 13 years ago I wrote a report on the road lobby. It has been out of print for more than ten years, and copies are now extremely hard to find. However, people keep on asking me for copies. My original idea was to update it, and revise the old text. In the end I decided to rewrite it completely, because so much has changed. This book has little in common with that first report, only the title stays the same. I couldn't think of a better one.

This book draws heavily on my experience in pressure groups during the 1970s, when I was often working in opposition to the road lobby. Outsiders frequently do not appreciate just how ludicrously easy changing policy can be – or on other occasions how impossibly difficult. The reason for this difference, that the ease of changing policy is directly related to the quality of the opposition to change, is the basic theme running through this book.

During this investigation I offered the British Road Federation a chance to state its case and to comment on the arguments in this book. Peter Witt, the BRF's director declined to see me, saying through a press officer that he did not think an interview would be worthwhile. Some others in the road lobby also followed the BRF's lead. What have they got to hide?

Illustrations

Figure

Abbreviations

AA	Automobile Association
BACMI	British Aggregate Construction Materials Industries
BRF	British Road Federation
CBI	Confederation of British Industry
FTA	Freight Transport Association
GLC	Greater London Council
RAC	Royal Automobile Club
RHA	Road Haulage Association
RIA	Roads Improvement Association
SMMT	Society of Motor Manufacturers and Traders

Notes

1 The Ministry of Transport became the Ministry of Transport and Civil Aviation in 1953, and then reverted to the Ministry of Transport in 1959. In 1970 it became part of the Department of the Environment. In 1976 it was renamed the Department of Transport. The 'ministry' refers to the Ministry of Transport in all its guises before 1976. The 'department' refers to the Department of Transport.

2 Before 1983 the weight limits for lorries were laid down in imperial tons. Since 1983 the legal limits have been metric tonnes. The difference between the two is small. An imperial ton is 1.6 per cent heavier than a metric tonne.

1 Introduction

The shape of Britain's motorway network was effectively decided at a closed meeting of the road lobby, towards the end of the Second World War. The meeting adopted a common goal of 1,000 miles of motorway. The first motorway opened in 1958. The first 1,000 miles were completed, ahead of schedule, in 1971.

Two years after that first crucial meeting, another private road lobby gathering discussed the lorry of the future. This group decided to push for a 40-tonne juggernaut. By 1983, and after considerable controversy, the maximum weight of heavy lorries was raised to 38 tonnes. One year later an administrative sleight of hand raised the maximum weight that could travel on Britain's roads without fear of prosecution to 40 tonnes.

In 1971 the road lobby again sat down to discuss a new motorway target. This time the goal was 3,000 miles. A few weeks later the government announced its plans, which were only marginally different from the road lobby's demands. So far about 1,800 miles of motorway have been built.[1]

Now an even more inflated target is being discussed, with talk of spending an extra £1.5 billion on major new road building in London. This plan includes four new roads to replace the ringways, abandoned back in the 1970s.

This book is about the road lobby. In the shadowy world of pressure groups the road lobby is the most powerful alliance of its kind. Yet it consists of no more than a few dozen active people. Over the years these people have moulded Britain's transport policy to suit the vested interests that back the road lobby, notably the motor industry and the road makers.

The road lobby has a remarkable list of achievements. Heavier lorries are here. The road building programme continues apace, with no sign of stopping. The road lobby has even fashioned a compliant government ministry to assist its aims, the Department of Transport.

Few would claim that Britain's transport policy is a success story.

Certainly the queues of passengers, waiting for buses that never seem to come, would not. Nor would the villages that have to bear the brunt of the new, heavier lorries. Nor would the settlements beset by a major new motorway. Nor would many pedestrians and cyclists. Six of them die every day under the wheels of motor vehicles.[2] Even Britain's 16 million motorists have plenty to complain about. It is no fun being stuck in a traffic jam, or being tailgated by a juggernaut on a motorway.

Britain's transport policy is designed to smooth the way for motor traffic. In the mid-1980s the government was spending about £1 billion building new motorways and other roads. In round figures, local councils spend another £1 billion on their new roads. In all, public expenditure on new roads was more than five times the investment in public transport, a figure which excludes another £1 billion spent on road maintenance.[3]

This pattern of spending reverses the usual social priorities. Private cars occupy most of Britain's road space. People who own cars tend to be well off. In the richest 10 per cent of the population, nine out of ten households have cars. In the poorest 10 per cent only one in ten has cars.[4]

About 40 per cent of Britain's households do not have a car at all. They are often people on supplementary benefit, the elderly or single parents. But even in those households which do have a car many people still depend on public transport, to a greater or lesser extent, simply because there are not enough cars to go round. Averaged over the whole country there is one car for every three people.

About four out of ten journeys are made by car.[5] The rest are mostly made on foot or by public transport. The government does, grudgingly, provide a subsidy to keep the buses and trains running. It is around £1.5 billion a year, approximately the same size as the subsidy given to drivers of company cars.[6] In 1986 the government intended to cut the subsidy to public transport substantially.

Traffic fumes and noise are part of everyday life in Britain's towns and cities. So too is danger. About 15 people die on the roads every day. Most people know of a friend or acquaintance who has died this way. More Britons have now died on the roads since 1940 than were killed during the Second World War on active service.[7]

By international standards, Britain's transport policy is noticeably pro-road. Most countries in Europe and the western world have had an increase in motoring over the last ten years. Most countries have also seen an increase in bus and train travel. Only five countries (out of a sample of twenty-two) have bucked this trend: Belgium, Denmark, Greece, Japan – and Great Britain.[8]

There is a similar story to be told about freight traffic. In most countries the railways are carrying less freight than they did ten years ago, although this has generally been a fairly gentle decline. In Britain rail freight dropped by a quarter over this decade. Only three countries had a sharper drop: Japan, Denmark and Luxembourg.[9]

Meanwhile business was booming for Britain's juggernauts. Several countries (including Britain) have seen a drop in goods leaving the factories and warehouses, which is scarcely surprising in a recession. But Britain was unique. Its lorry traffic went up at the same time as tonnage was falling.[10]

One of the best touchstones of policy is the way a government spends its money, or conversely the way it chooses to save money. Britain has not been alone in building motorways. Over the last twenty years all of the countries in western Europe have built motorways, but only one country, France, has expanded its motorway network at a faster rate than Britain.[11]

Britain has been second to none in its enthusiasm for running down public transport. The easiest indicator is the mileage of railway network because this reflects both public transport and freight policies.

Not many countries have built new railways over the last twenty years, and most have closed more lines than they have opened. What marks out Britain from the rest is the sheer extent of its closures. Britain has ripped up 37 per cent of its railways, more than Luxembourg (31 per cent), the United States (24 per cent) and twenty-three other European countries. [12]

Not surprisingly Britain has been backward at investing in its railways. Most countries have pursued a policy of railway electrification. By 1983 Britain had electrified 22 per cent of its railways, a figure which had been inflated by the closures of the previous twenty years, which had concentrated on lines which had not been electrified. Fifteen countries had electrified a higher proportion of their railways. Only five had electrified a lower proportion – East Germany, Portugal, Denmark, Greece and Ireland.

Of course there are explanations, at least in part, for some of these trends. Britain was late to start building motorways and so might be expected to expand its network quickly.

It was the first country to build railways. So perhaps wasteful competition in the nineteenth century led to unnecessary lines being built, which were long overdue for closure. Maybe, as one civil servant in the Department of Transport argued, Britain is too small a country for rail freight to thrive.

Or is there some hidden hand guiding transport policy? What part does the road lobby play in forming policy? After all, none of these trends runs counter to its interests.

One of the road lobby's main aims is to 'separate roads from the general ruck of social expenditure'.[13] Or, as one of the lobby's senior figures put it in rather more graphic terms:

> We do not say that other things are less important but however much money you spend on fighting illness there is no certainty that the germs will get any less active, whereas if you spend more money on road congestion, the cost of road congestion will reduce.[14]

Certainly road investment has become remarkably immune to spending cuts. Although the plans were trimmed slightly during the late 1970s, the road builders have enjoyed nearly thirty years of steady growth, easily outstripping other spending programmes, such as new houses, hospitals, schools or even sewers.[15]

In 1986 Nicholas Ridley, who was then Secretary of State for Transport, boasted that spending on new roads had increased by 26 per cent, over and above the rate of inflation, since the Conservatives were elected in 1979.[16] That is a bigger increase than any other spending programme, with the sole exception of social security, although roads, unlike defence and law and order, were not a major plank in the election platform for either 1979 or 1983.

The road lobby itself is understandably ambivalent about its success. On the one hand, it is keen to claim credit where it is due (and sometimes where it is not), because the lobbyists' jobs depend on their continuing success. Thus, in 1978, the British Road Federation, one of the central groups in the lobby, was awarded the Castrol Gold Medal by the Institute of the Motor Industry for its 'outstanding advocacy'. The medal is awarded for 'the greatest contribution . . . to the advancement of the cause of road transport'.[17]

On other occasions the lobby is keen to play down its influence, lest it attract unwelcome public attention. So one year after the BRF won its gold medal, a lobby leader denied the existence of 'a massive road lobby. I only wish there were'.[18]

The simplest way out of this welter of claims and counter claims is to turn to politicians, who have to bear the brunt of the road lobby's pressure, for a more impartial assessment. The road lobby is not the only grouping of its kind. The nuclear power industry, the agricultural lobby, the record companies (campaigning for a levy on cassette tapes) and many other lobbies continually pace the corridors of power.

The politicians are virtually unanimous in their praise for the road lobby. Frank Allaun, who was a Labour backbencher until 1983, said that the BRF was 'the strongest lobby inside parliament'[19] echoing the words of another backbencher, back in 1960.[20]

In 1985, Denis Healey said that when he was Chancellor of the Exchequer the strongest pressure on him came from the 'motor lobby'.[21] While Norman Fowler, speaking as Conservative transport spokesman, just a few weeks before becoming Secretary of State for Transport, said 'anyone who's had anything to do with the kind of research the BRF have done, whether they agree with them or not, would actually recognise their expertise . . .'[22]. Albert Booth, who was Labour's front bench spokesman on transport until the 1983 election, concurred. Booth, who was no friend of the road lobby, said: 'It was very much a professional organisation. It undoubtedly had a lot of money, had very good research, its publicity was good and its publications superb.'[23]

Barbara Castle also testifies to the strength of the lobby:

When I took over as Minister of Transport the most vociferous lobby in this country was that represented by road interests. The propaganda and pressure groups led by the British Road Federation said we must concentrate all our resources on building the first 1,000 miles of motorway. The environment lobby had barely been born, and when I tried to suggest that there were other considerations that we should bear in mind I had an uphill task because the whole of public opinion and the then opposition were against me.[24]

Castle's point is fundamental to the link between pressure groups and policy. The reason she was under pressure was the lack of any opposition to the road lobby.

Policy is the resolution of conflicting pressures, as an American journalist, Art Bentley, pointed out nearly eighty years ago.[25] Transport policy is no exception. Indeed, in the case of transport policy the definition can be drawn even tighter. The only pressures that count come from pressure groups and the civil service.

Transport rarely figures as an issue in elections. The four main exceptions in recent years have all been local examples. In 1973, Labour won the GLC elections, gaining votes by its pledge to abolish a system of urban motorways, known as the ringways. In 1981 Labour's pledge to cut bus and tube fares in London again helped it to win votes.

In 1986, the Liberal Party produced a by-election upset when it won the safe Tory seat of Ryedale. One of the reasons for the upset was that voters were worried that the 1985 Transport Act would jeopardise the future of rural buses. While in the council elections of 1986, anti-road votes put Labour into power in the Lothian Region, because of Labour's promise to stop a controversial road in Edinburgh. The swings to Labour were markedly higher in wards affected by the road plan.[26]

These are exceptions. Normally transport is not an issue at elections, and certainly not general elections. If votes do not count, transport ministers can afford to ignore public opinion. They do, regularly. The maximum weight of heavy lorries, for example, was raised (albeit somewhat nervously) in the face of overwhelming opposition from public opinion.

In 1986, the Department of Transport canvassed public opinion in London about four major new roads which it wanted to build. The survey in East London found that 90 per cent of the public wanted better public transport instead.[27] The government had halved the subsidy to London's buses and tubes, in just three years from 1983 to 1986, and cut the bus service. The people who carried out the survey for the government argued that 'it was not a head count'.[28]

With voters largely excluded from influencing transport policy, the pressures on government are the result of the various lobbies' activities. But the road lobby does have its opponents. The environment lobby has grown considerably in strength and sophistication since Barbara Castle left the Ministry of Transport in 1969. The railways and the buses also have some influence on policy.

Finally, the road lobby often has to compete indirectly with other lobbies. In its fight to have more money spent on roads the road lobby may be able to persuade the department of its case. But the department then has to fight the case for more money against the competing claims put up by other government departments, and at second hand, by their lobbies.

The road lobby's great advantage is that the Department of Transport is firmly committed to the cause. The road lobby is not the only pressure group to enjoy a close relationship with a government department. The nuclear power lobby has its links with the Department of Energy. But what makes the partnership between the road lobby and the Department of Transport unique is its outstanding record of success.

The major problem in analysing the activity of any pressure group is that the majority of the evidence is circumstantial. Rarely is there a smoking gun. The road lobby calls for a new road; the environmentalists protest (don't they always); the department decides; and a road is built. The sequence of events is clear, and the inference obvious. But it falls short of incontrovertible proof, which would be to show that the road lobby, or its allies in the department, had a decisive influence on this sequence of events.

The main actors, from ministers downwards, are often unaware of the parts played by others, or at least the full extent of their parts. Indeed it is part of the lobbyists' art to disguise the full extent of a lobby's role, and to make approaches through third parties. Witnesses may choose to inflate (or play down) their role, and in any case memories fade as time passes.

Independent sources are hard to find. Sometimes a civil servant gives a glimpse through the shroud of official secrecy by leaking a document to a newspaper or pressure group.

The most complete source is the historical records released by the government under the thirty-year rule. Some are too out of date to be relevant. Some essential files have been weeded and destroyed, including one of the most important files relating to the birth of the motorway network.[29]

Fortunately for researchers, all of the road lobby's major achievements are the results of continuing campaigns, going back many years. The campaign for heavier lorries started more than forty years ago. The motorway campaign goes back fifty years, into the mists of missing files. The moulding of a ministry in the road lobby's own image goes back more than sixty years.

2 Inside the road lobby

The road lobby is a network of vested interests: the people who make the cars that clog the roads; the people who fuel these cars; the people who build the roads to relieve the traffic jams (and create them a few miles down the road); the people who own the lorries that cause the roads to crumble; and the people who patch them up. The road lobby exists for the sole purpose of influencing government policy, so that it can sell more cars, lorries, oil, rubber and concrete.

On its most superficial level, the road lobby is an alliance of trade associations, the groups set up to promote a particular industrial sector, such as the Cement and Concrete Association. Trade associations often provide common services for an industry, by collaborating on research or training. But their most important function is to negotiate with government on behalf of their industries, and to lobby politicians. Trade associations have mostly been around for so long that they are often not recognised for what they are – pressure groups.[1]

Behind the trade associations that support the road lobby are some of the biggest and most powerful companies in Britain, and the world. The three biggest companies in the world, in terms of turnover, are Exxon (Esso), Shell and General Motors. All three have been active supporters of the road lobby. Six out of the top ten companies in the world are either oil companies or motor manufacturers.[2] They wield vast power.[3]

Britain's top two firms are both oil companies, BP and Shell. Four oil companies figure in the top ten companies. Although motor manufacturing has declined in importance in the last decade, Ford is still Britain's nineteenth largest company, by turnover, and British Leyland (now Rover) is twenty-second largest.[4]

The road lobby has five main sources of support. Four of these are the main industries. The fifth source is the motoring clubs, the AA and the RAC. The most important supporter of the road lobby is the motor industry. Its natural allies are the people who use its products,

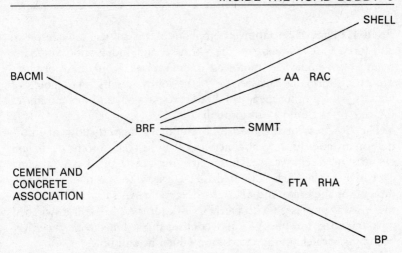

1 The main links in the road lobby

the motoring clubs and the lorry operators. The two other sectors of
support are the oil industry and the road makers. But the road lobby
does not just consist of big business. Its tentacles stretch into county
halls throughout the land, and into the Department of Transport.

The easiest starting point for a tour of the road lobby is the BRF,
which was founded in 1932 as the 'one representative body which is
making efforts to combat the sinister and distorted propaganda of
the railways in their efforts to enslave British industry'.[5] The BRF has
close links with all the industrial supporters of the road lobby. But it is
far from synonymous with the road lobby, just one of the constituents.

The BRF has two main roles. The first is to campaign for more
road building. In the past, the BRF had a much wider remit. The first
stage of the campaign against the nationalisation of road haulage in
1945–6, for instance, was conducted by the BRF 'on behalf of the
road haulage industry'.[6]

However, since the mid-1960s the BRF's activities have been limited
to pushing for more road building.

Its second role is to provide a forum for the road lobby, through
its committee meetings. Both inside and outside these meetings the
various factions in the road lobby can come together and coordinate
their strategy and tactics. The opportunity provided by these meetings
for people in the road lobby to get to know one another is one of
the major factors in the cohesiveness of this alliance.

Only on a handful of occasions in recent years has this unity
cracked. In 1972, for example, the AA and the RAC added their
voices to the public protests about juggernauts. The hurt tone of the

Road Haulage Association's complaint is revealing: 'a widespread anti-lorry lobby which, to the surprise and indignation of many members, includes the motoring organisations'.[7] But these disputes are rare. Normally each sector of the lobby has its own sphere of activity, which other members do not trespass on, and this minimises the risk of any falling out in public.

The closeness of the road lobby, and the smooth flow of information around this 'old boy' network, can be seen in some of the job changes in recent years. Thus when the AA wanted a new chief executive in 1964 it headhunted Alec Durie, who was then managing director of Shell-mex and BP. According to the AA's official historian,[8] the AA was impressed with Durie's work for the BRF. Durie switched jobs to work for the AA, and continued his links with the BRF, becoming vice-chairman, a position which he still holds.

The present director of the BRF is Peter Witt, a Yorkshireman. Described by a former colleague as having 'a gentlemanly air' which conceals 'a hard line politician', Witt joined the BRF in 1985 after many years of service with the Cement and Concrete Association.

Witt's predecessor in the top job at the BRF was the lanky and languid David Gent, who joined the BRF from the SMMT in 1983, and left to become the chief executive of the Motor Agents' Association. Before Gent was the golf-loving Ken Cannell, who had been deputy director since the 1960s, before taking the main job in 1981. Cannell left to join Ford, another BRF member.

Robert Phillipson, director of the BRF for twenty of its most important years, left in 1981 to head the newly-formed BACMI, yet another BRF member. Phillipson, whose fondness for listening to jazz at Ronnie Scott's club is not always shared by the beneficiaries of the expense account, also worked for a BRF member before becoming director.[9]

The BRF's membership has been declining in recent years. Individuals cannot join the BRF, so all its members are corporate, either companies or trade associations. Between 1977 and 1985 the number of members fell from 175 to 140. Some of these losses were the consequence of members merging with others. Many were caused by the resignation of associate members who contributed little towards the cost of running the BRF.

However, two of the losses were damaging. In 1977, the BRF lost an annual income of £5,000 when Vauxhall pulled out. It suffered another blow in 1985 when Esso, one of its major backers, withdrew. Nevertheless with an income of £340,000 in 1985, the BRF is still a very well-financed pressure group.[10]

The main seat of power in the BRF is its executive committee. All the main financial supporters of the BRF have a place on this committee, except the Society of Motor Manufacturers and Traders, which has two. One of its representatives is Sam Toy, who was the SMMT's president in 1986 and 1987 as well as being chairman and managing director of Ford. He is one of the most influential members of this committee.

The SMMT is the biggest single contributor to the BRF, providing roughly 20 per cent of its income.[11] The SMMT itself has a turnover of £3 million. It is not just a pressure group. It organises the Motor Show and finances research, both at the Motor Industry Research Association, at Nuneaton, and by sponsoring a chair of motor industry economics, at University College Cardiff.[12]

The motor industry's interest in the road lobby is to enable it to sell more cars and lorries. In the words of Lord Stokes, a former chairman of British Leyland and a past president of the SMMT: 'in the end my job is to make money for the shareholders through selling cars, and everything else is ancillary to that . . .'[13]

The SMMT chooses to cloak the motive with national interest by reworking the dictum 'what is good for the country is good for General Motors, and what is good for General Motors is good for the country' for local consumption.[14]

What happens to the motor industry and its products in the next few years will make Britain a better or worse place to live. For

1 *Forbes House, the SMMT's £3 million headquarters among the embassies of London's Belgravia*

the health of the economy is inextricably linked to the health of the motor industry.[15]

The industry generally opposes any limit on the use of vehicles and any increase in taxation, lest it reduce sales. It supports road building because faster roads make its products more attractive, and because traffic congestion makes cars and lorries less useful.

In recent years, the SMMT has fought to keep lead in petrol and to prevent motor manufacturers from being forced to install catalytic converters in their cars to cut exhaust pollution. In 1986 the SMMT was still campaigning to have the 10 per cent tax on new cars removed, arguing that without the tax sales would rise above 2 million and help the domestic motor industry compete with Europe and Japan.

In 1984 the SMMT launched a 'motor industry promotion campaign'. In 1985 the campaign cost nearly £450,000. It is designed for an industry that spends £160 million on advertising its products, 'to obtain a better understanding from politicians, the media and eventually the general public of the importance of the motor industry to the nation's economy and our way of life'.[16]

The campaign has two main aims; cutting taxes and increasing road building. It has one motive: selling more cars, or as the SMMT puts it:

> The British tax system discriminates against the motor vehicle and thus places an extra burden on the motor industry. Our inadequate road system restricts the use, enjoyment and cost-effectiveness of motoring and causes unnecessary inconvenience. These are the two main reasons for Britain's lower level of car ownership than in comparable countries and the UK car population is thus well short of its potential size.[17]

Shell and BP both have seats on the BRF's executive committee, as did Esso until its resignation. Since the 1973–4 oil crisis, the major oil companies have become even more dependent on transport, and principally road transport, for their profits, with the price rises forcing a cutback in the use of oil for heating.

Between 1973 and 1985 Shell's sales of its major oil products in the domestic market halved. But its sales of fuel for transport (the vast majority of which is for road transport) increased by a third. Transport fuels now account for three-quarters of its sales of major products.[18]

In addition the company sells lubricating oils for motor vehicles, and bitumen, which is used for road surfacing and making asphalt.

Shell supplied more than 60 per cent of the bitumen used in the M25, London's orbital motorway. What is good for the motor industry is also good for the oil companies.

The construction industry also has a natural interest in the road lobby. The chief trade associations are BACMI and the Cement and Concrete Association. About 80 per cent of Britain's roads are made of asphalt, and probably by a BACMI member; the other 20 per cent are made of concrete.

BACMI was founded in 1981 as a result of the merger of three trade associations.[19] This is a £2 billion a year industry. BACMI members supply roughly 90 per cent of asphalt and crushed rock, about 60 per cent of sand and gravel and half of ready mixed concrete sold in Britain.

BACMI, which in 1985 had a turnover of more than £700,000, is one of the BRF's more prominent supporters. In 1981 it gave the BRF £23,000. Its chief executive is Robert Phillipson.

The Cement and Concrete Association, which had a turnover of £6 million in 1985, has been a long-standing supporter of the BRF. Most of its activities are concerned with training and research although it spends a fair amount of effort in politicking. Peter Witt was in charge of this side of the Association's activities until he moved to the BRF. The Association has a membership of three.[20]

Several individual road building companies, all with wider construction interests, are members of the BRF, including McAlpine, Tarmac and Wimpey. The attraction for construction companies of building roads is that the contracts are fairly risk free. The government (or county council) is unlikely to go bust halfway through. And unlike house building, a new road is not going to hang around unsold.

The lorry operators have two trade associations, the Freight Transport Association and the Road Haulage Association. The division between the two goes back to the old system of licensing lorries, which was abandoned in 1968. The members of the FTA are firms like Marks and Spencer, which distribute their wares by lorry. The RHA's members, however, operate for hire or reward, to use the old licensing terminology. Road hauliers will carry anyone's goods, at a price.

The FTA's chief executive, Garry Turvey, has a seat on the BRF's executive committee. The FTA is considerably more wealthy than the RHA, with a turnover of £5 million in 1984, compared with the RHA's £1.2 million.[21] Both associations provide common services for their industry, such as training and vehicle inspection. Both are closely involved in lobbying.

The FTA continually tries to present itself as neutral between road and rail. Every press release, for example, carries the image-balancing claim that FTA members are 'responsible for over 90 per cent of the freight carried by British Rail'. But the bulk of its political activity is concerned with road transport. This goes back to the FTA's formation in 1969 as a result of a merger between three trade associations. The dominant body was the Traders' Road Transport Association. The same press releases that proclaim the FTA's interest in rail freight also give the game away. They are about road freight, almost without exception, and frequently promote the FTA's aim to increase the maximum lorry weight. Out of fifty press releases issued by the FTA in the first half of 1986, only one was about rail freight.

The recession has restricted the lorry operators' opportunities for growth. Their main strategy has two parts. First, to increase their market share by encouraging freight to switch from rail to road. And second, to encourage the replacement of local distribution systems with more centralised ones, geared to the motorway network, so that the output of the lorries can rise even though the volume of goods remains restricted.

The main targets of both the FTA and the RHA have been to increase the maximum weight of lorries and to raise the motorway mileage. Heavier lorries can help to cut the cost of road freight (when they are full), as can motorways, because of their higher speed limits. This helps to shift the competitive balance away from rail and in favour of roads, making it possible to centralise distribution still further.

Similarly lorry operators are keen to prevent any further restriction on lorry use. They fervently oppose any ban on lorries using local streets, have argued for laxer restrictions on drivers' hours, and campaigned against tachographs, which keep an automatic check on how long drivers are at the wheel.

Although the FTA has mounted highly effective campaigns against the night time ban on lorries in London, for example, neither association is well thought of by others in the road lobby. One source in the lobby described the FTA as 'bludgeoning people over the head before trying to reason with them'.

The AA and the RAC are both keen supporters of the road lobby. Both are represented on the BRF's executive. In addition the BRF has two vice-chairmen, one from the AA and one from the RAC.

The RAC is the smaller of the two clubs. About 1.5 million motorists 'belong' to the RAC. But they are only associate members, and have no voting rights. Only the RAC's 15,000 full members have the vote. But even they have relatively little power to influence the way the club is run. The club's rules, which were last changed in 1979, mean that the power of voters to change policy is quite restricted.[22]

Effectively the RAC is run by a committee of sixteen men. Every three years, five of the committee have to stand for re-election. Anyone wanting to break into this committee has to submit nomination papers two months in advance of the annual general meeting.

The RAC has a well-merited reputation for being more politically backward than the AA. The club still hankers after the 1930s image of the open road, where a chap out for a run might barely see another car. The world has changed. The RAC has not.

A clue to the motivation for this outlook is contained in the club's rules, which specifically state that directors do not have to retire when they reach the age of 70. And somewhat coy the directors are – for they do not have to declare their age. When the RAC last published the age of most of its directors, which was back in 1974, only three were born this century.[23]

On the surface the AA, with a membership of 6 million, is more democratic than the RAC. All its members are equal: none has a vote. The AA is run by a committee which is self-selecting.

In the late 1960s the AA came in for considerable criticism for not taking a tougher line over the small print exclusions in car guarantees. The root of the problem was the AA's aims, including 'protecting and advancing the legitimate interests of the motor industry', which effectively stifled any criticisms of the industry.[24]

Matters came to a head at the 1968 annual general meeting. Despite the defence of the AA's chairman, Lord Brentford, 'we fight the industry very violently',[25] the challenge was effectively thwarted by packing the meeting with the AA's staff, according to one observer.[26]

The AA changed its rules, dropping the contentious aim of supporting the motor industry, in 1971. The AA circulated its membership beforehand, telling its members, then numbering 4 million, that it intended to change the rules – but not telling them what the changes were. Only eighty-five members turned up at the meeting. One protested at the 'antiquated, inefficient and totally inadequate' method of informing members, saying that it gave the impression of a 'sordid and squalid manoeuvre to obscure the facts'. The protest was in vain.[27]

All the AA's staff automatically become members of the association. The annual general meetings are usually held at the Savoy Hotel, in London. A mid-week meeting is scarcely designed to encourage the participation of ordinary members, although it is doubtless more convenient for full-time staff. Normally only a few dozen members turn up – including staff.

Nevertheless the AA is more progressive than the RAC. In 1975, two women were appointed to the ruling committee, for the first time ever. The AA's official history describes it as 'a revolutionary step'.[28]

In addition to supporting the BRF, the motoring clubs also have their own coordinating body, the Standing Joint Committee. This committee, which was set up in 1944, has three members: the AA, the RAC and their Scottish counterpart, the Royal Scottish Automobile Club.

The motoring clubs pursue a broad policy of opposing any restrictions on car use, opposing bus lanes, reducing motoring taxes and calling for increased road spending. They pursue these aims both through the BRF, their own committee, and individually.

The club's attitude to taxation is so long term and consistent that any catalogue of all the different attempts to prevent tax increases would be tedious. Before every budget, the Chancellor of the Exchequer has to face demands not to increase petrol tax, or the licence duty, as regular as the first cuckoo of spring.

Two more general campaigns have been the AA's 1969 'square deal' campaign – a phrase echoing the railways' pre-war publicity – which was a demand for more road spending and lower motoring taxation.[29] In 1981 the RAC introduced a campaign on the same theme, this time called 'close the gap'.[30]

Both the AA and the RAC frequently oppose curbs on the use of cars, from campaigning against the 70 mph speed limit in 1967 (the AA wanted only an advisory limit) to their success in preventing random breath testing of drunken drivers in the same year. The AA has now modified its opposition to random tests.[31]

The clubs frequently claim to represent Britain's motorists, although members have scant say in the policies that the clubs pursue, and indeed little interest. A 1976 survey of AA members found that 93 per cent joined because of the breakdown service. The second most important service to members was the legal defence. In a total of fifteen services provided by the AA, ranging from its handbook to the travel service, the political activities were not even mentioned.[32]

This lack of democracy has produced internal dissent in the past. In 1975 Lt Col Gerald Haythornethwaite, an AA member for forty years, resigned in protest at the AA's support for a motorway through the Peak District.[33]

The AA's response was to set up a panel of motorists, which it consults over political and other issues, to try to ensure that it does not get out of touch with its members. Although this is a long way short of democracy, these polls of members views have produced a pronounced softening of the AA's views in recent times. This has been most noticeable over the AA's attitude to random breath testing. Its polls showed that members would support measures which saved lives.[34]

Although most of this politicking is carried on in the name of members, most motorists seem to be more or less apathetic. A number of attempts have been made to set up a pressure group for motorists. None has taken root.

The bus industry's support for the road lobby is on the wane. It is largely an historical relic, a throwback to the days before the Second World War when lorry owners and bus companies made common cause against the powerful railway lobby. Today the railway lobby has lost much of its power, and the rivalry between bus and train has largely subsided.

The bus industry has now much more in common with the railways. And the road lobby is more of a threat than a friend. The commercial incentive for the road lobby to favour cars, rather than buses, is quite clear. In the mid-1980s, a double decker bus would cost about £70,000 – or £1,000 a seat. A four-seater car might easily cost £8,000 – or £2,000 a seat. The motor industry's natural commercial interest is to make cars and not buses. Any successful effort to promote buses could easily undermine the industry's car sales, the biggest and most profitable part of its output.

So while the SMMT is energetic in its defence of the motor car it does little to help the bus. In 1987, the SMMT expects bus sales to be less than half of what they were in 1984.[35] The collapse of the bus market is largely a result of the 1985 Transport Act, which jeopardises the long-term future of many bus routes by introducing deregulation. Consequently few operators have been buying buses. The bus operators opposed the legislation, vigorously, but without the support of the SMMT.

The main trade association for the bus industry, the Bus and Coach Council, is a member of the BRF, but it contributes relatively little financially, about £500 a year at the beginning of the 1980s. The state-owned National Bus Company resigned from the BRF in July 1986. The Bus and Coach Council did have discussions about joining Transport 2000, the avidly pro-public transport pressure group, which is a deadly rival of the BRF, but talks broke down in 1983.

For the road lobby, the main advantage of the bus industry's continued involvement is political. The BRF unashamedly uses the bus industry as window dressing. Thus, in a letter to political party leaders just before the 1974 general election, the BRF claimed to represent a wide spectrum of road users. It picked out nine of its members, including the two nationalised bus companies, to illustrate this point[36].

The BRF works closely with the Roads Campaign Council, a body which was set up in 1955, largely at the initiative of the SMMT. The SMMT was keen to involve the motoring clubs more closely. Neither the AA nor the RAC was then a member of the BRF.

The initial letter which was sent to likely supporters was signed by the AA, the RAC and the SMMT, jointly.[37] The council was launched at a lunch at the Savoy Hotel in 1955.[38] Its inaugural press conference was not held until a fortnight later, this time at the Waldorf Hotel.[39] The council united the motoring clubs, with the bus and lorry operators, the SMMT and the BRF. Its aim was to restore to motoring the freedom it was losing because of congestion – or, as the *Manchester Guardian* wrote, 'putting votes into roads'.[40]

The council hired Aims of Industry (now just called Aims) to run its publicity. The man who then ran this right-wing pressure group, Roger Sewill, had previously run the campaign against the nationalisation of road haulage when he was at the RHA.[41]

The council ran an aggressive campaign for motorway building. It published its own broadsheet 'Highway Times', which achieved a distribution of about 100,000 copies.[42] However, in 1963 the council split, following a bizarre internal row. The AA and the SMMT went off to join the BRF, while the RAC and the Motor Agents' Association (the trade association for garages) stuck with the Roads Campaign Council. These four groups had been the financial power behind the council, each contributing £7,500 towards its costs. Some of this money ended up in the BRF's pockets, because the council employed the BRF to research its case.[43]

The BRF also withdrew from the council, making a coded reference to the row.

> The federation remains a member. . . . From the end of October, however, it ceased to be represented on any of the council's committees. . . . During the year the federation continued to provide such information and services as were required. Whilst there has been no formal cancellation of this arrangement it has not been renewed for 1964.[44]

The cause of the split goes back to the curious case of an unauthorised 'no parking' sign posted on railings outside a house which the Minister of Transport, Ernest Marples, owned. The council published a picture of the sign in its broadsheet[45] saying it was outside the Minister's home. The broadsheet gently jeered at the Minister. The picture and story were eventually picked up by the national press.

Marples became very annoyed, and put pressure on the Roads Campaign Council to print an apology. After some initial resistance the council caved in, and duly printed a grovelling note, saying that the sign was on the house next door.[46]

All of which was slightly unfair to the poor council. Although the apology was not wrong, Marples also owned the house next door, a fact which the council successfully prevented from becoming public knowledge.[47]

When the split came, the *Daily Telegraph* explained it by saying that the council had 'undoubtedly irritated successive ministers of transport'.[48] The split was formally patched up in 1970 when the Roads Campaign Council was, in the BRF's word, 'reconstituted'.[49] The council's chairman, Jack Williams, a leading figure in the RAC, was given a place at the BRF's executive committee. The RAC formally joined the BRF in 1973.

Today the Roads Campaign Council is the parliamentary arm of the BRF. The council runs the parliamentary All Party Roads Study Group, which it set up in 1957. It is run by Arthur Butler, a mild and inoffensive public relations man who used to be the political correspondent of the *Daily Sketch*, from the city offices of Charles Barker. Charles Barker, a firm which specialises in parliamentary lobbying and which has a turnover of more than £1 million, also handles the accounts of the FTA and the SMMT.

In 1969 the SMMT, backed by the RAC, set up the British Industry Roads Campaign as 'a money raising fund for the BRF'. This campaign was a trust fund, with an anticipated life of fourteen years, initially designed to raise funds for the 1970 general election campaign. The trustees pledged themselves 'to concentrate on giving the fullest support to the British Road Federation's programme for 1970'.[50]

The fund was initially successful. It attracted the support of about fifty companies, mostly in the motor industry. In its first year of operation, 1970, the industry channelled £60,000 into the BRF, doubling its income.[51] But its contributions to the BRF began to tail off as early as 1971, and the campaign was wound up halfway through its life span in 1976.

Again the SMMT consulted its members 'on plans to maintain and expand the essential work which the BRF does to support the case for a positive attitude towards the road vehicles on the part of national and local government and the general public'.[52] The SMMT circulated its members with a recommended list of subscriptions rates, geared to company turnover.[53] But this produced no tangible results, indeed Vauxhall pulled out of the BRF in 1977.

The CBI is also active in support of the road lobby, frequently joining in delegations from the road lobby to see ministers and supporting the BRF's local groups. The CBI's transport committee has a high degree of overlap with the membership of the FTA. In July 1986 the chairman of this committee, as he had been for more than five years, was Len Payne, a director of the supermarket firm Sainsbury. From 1980 to 1982, Payne was president of the FTA, subsequently becoming treasurer, a post which he held until 1985.[54]

The BRF, like most pressure groups, is studiously neutral in its politics. It makes no political donations, as it sententiously points out in its annual reports. But its members do. In 1985 a score of the BRF's members, firms such as Tarmac and Taylor Woodrow, contributed £280,000 to the Conservative Party – and £10,000 to the Alliance.[55]

The BRF has always instinctively allied itself with the right. When it was first set up, one senior lobbyist described the organising committee in a letter to Conservative Central Office as 'almost entirely Conservative in its political composition'.[56]

Beyond the business interests and the motoring clubs the road lobby also has the support of other factions. The most important of these is the engineers who survey, design and plan roads. Some of these are employed by local councils, normally in the offices of the county surveyors, and some are employed by the Department of Transport.

The county surveyors themselves have their own pressure group, the County Surveyors' Society, which celebrated its centenary in 1985 and has an influence out of all proportion to its rather meagre income, which in the early 1980s was running at under £1,000 a year.

The society has played an active part in drawing up plans for future road building. It provides transport advice to the Association of County Councils, and its members also advise the Association of Metropolitan Authorities.

Road engineers also belong to two professional bodies, the Institution of Civil Engineers and the Institution of Highways and Transportation, which before 1980 was called the Institution of Highway Engineers. Neither body is as overt as the BRF in pushing the road lobby line. But both of them, in their more discreet style, have been pushing for more road building.

The great strength of the institutions is that many of their members are employed by the government. Thus when Ron Bridle stood for election to the Council of the Institution of Civil Engineers he called for 'better contact with influential sources in government, the civil services and industry to ensure that on issues affecting the membership and society at large professional skills and opinions are brought to bear'. At the time, Bridle was the Department of Transport's chief highway engineer.[57]

The civil engineers drew up a plan for a large increase in spending on infrastructure in 1983, much of which was to be spent on roads. The Government rejected the plan. Tony Gaffney, the county surveyor of West Yorkshire, who became president of the institution in 1984, said the rejection was a 'great shame'. He called for 'increased discussion at permanent secretary level rather than direct confrontation with the government'.[58]

By 1986, the civil engineers were becoming more impatient, although not quite to the point of dumping discretion in favour of direct action. One senior member, calling for higher road spending, said that the institution must adopt a higher profile as a pressure group. 'Some of the institution's proclamations will have political overtones as engineers will be competing with representatives from other sectors of society.'[59]

The road lobby, like the multinational companies that finance it, does not stop at national boundaries. The International Road Federation was founded in 1948, mainly at the instigation of the BRF and its French counterpart. It is based in Geneva and Washington and has eighty-nine affiliated members in countries around the world. When it was founded there were only eight member organisations.[60]

The Federation's main role is to push for international roads, such as the route from Cairo to the Cape in Africa. It enjoys consultative status with most international bodies, including the European Conference of Ministers of Transport and the Organisation of African Unity.

The Permanent International Association of Road Congresses is a curious collection of pressure groups and governments, paid for, in Britain, largely out of the public purse. It was founded in 1922 by William Rees Jeffreys, a notable road lobbyist, and reconstituted in its present form in 1948.

On the British committee are groups such as the BRF and the Institution of Highways and Transportation, as well as engineers from the Department of Transport. The department provides the secretariat, although as far back as the 1940s, civil service administrators were questioning why the public was paying for this association.[61]

Its main role is to disseminate information about road building, and politically it adopts the usual road lobby line of being reluctant to approve anything which restricts the flow of traffic.[62] Its main interest is that it is another illustration of the blurred line that barely exists between the road lobby and certain sections of the Department of Transport, notably the engineers. There is no equivalent organisation for rail transport. The department's explanation is that its membership 'stems from the department's executive responsibilities.

That there is no rail equivalent only reflects the different organisation and problems of the railways'.[63]

The other sectors of the road lobby have their own international organisations. The FTA, the RHA and the Bus and Coach Council are the British members of the International Road Transport Union, which was founded in 1948. Its aims are 'the promotion . . . of national and international road transport'.[64] While the motoring clubs belong to the World Touring and Automobile Association (the AA) or the Fédération Internationale de l'Automobile (the RAC).

The general consensus is that the British road lobby is as well organised and effective as that in any other country in the world, with the possible exception of the United States. In Washington, during the 1970s, the road lobby met every Thursday at the Lafayette Hotel.[65] Over lunch some fifty men coordinated their strategy. Their biggest coup was in the 1950s when the lobbyists dreamed up the Highway Trust Fund, which was financed by a tax on petrol. This tax financed the building of America's interstate freeways. It was not until twenty years later that the authorities were allowed to divert some of this fund into financing public transport.

The make-up of the American road lobby is much the same as the British. It comprises the makers of cars, tyres, roads, the oil companies and the people who used their products. In 1949 General Motors, Standard Oil of California and Firestone Tire were convicted under American anti-trust legislation of conspiring to replace electric trains, notably in Los Angeles, by buses. In 1973 a Senate Committee was told that General Motors systematically bought up urban railways and converted them to buses. 'By 1949, General Motors had been involved in the replacement of more than 100 electric transit systems with GM buses in forty-five cities.'[66] In reply, General Motors argued that the systems it bought were in decline anyway, and 'doomed . . . it did, however, through its buses help to alleviate the disruption left in their wake'.[67]

The Los Angeles railways finally closed in 1960. In 1985 the city approved a plan to rebuild one of the lines.

3 The growth of the road lobby

By a delicious irony, the road lobby was given its start by a combination of cyclists and environmentalists, two groups which are today among the road lobby's most dedicated opponents. The environmentalists were concerned about the clouds of dust produced by cyclists in the days before roads were metalled.

In response the two main cycling bodies, the Cyclists' Touring Club and the National Cyclists' Union, called a conference on the state of the nation's roads. It was held in Gloucester in April 1886. The conference decided to set up a new pressure group to press for better roads, the Roads Improvement Association. The two cycling bodies financed the RIA.[1]

Initially the RIA went around the country highlighting instances of poor maintenance. This agitation had its effect. In 1888 the Local Government Act made counties responsible for the main roads.

After this success the RIA ran out of steam. By 1892 it was in financial trouble and the NCU was becoming increasingly reluctant to part with its money. The RIA became moribund.[2]

In about 1897 the Cyclists' Touring Club decided to establish the RIA more firmly. The RIA was incorporated in 1898. In 1901 the RIA moved into offices just round the corner from Parliament, signalling the association's political intentions. It was still a shoestring operation, and the office furniture was lent by the Cyclists' Touring Club.[3] The tension between the two cycling bodies continued. In 1902 the club gave the RIA £71, on condition that the union contributed £50. The club noted with disgust in its minutes that the union only paid one guinea, and that came from one of its local groups.[4]

The abolition of the law forcing motor vehicles to have someone walking in front of them carrying a red flag, in 1896, created a new class with an interest in better roads – the automobilist. The first motoring clubs were not very prepossessing. The Motor Car Club was a promotional front for Harry Lawson, a shady motor industry financier, the John de Lorean of his day.[5] But the club did organise the first London to Brighton run to celebrate the abolition of the red flag, which survives today as the veteran cars' run.

In 1897, the secretary of Lawson's club left to set up the Automobile Club which, since 1907, has been called the Royal Automobile Club. The newly formed club wanted to affiliate to the Cyclists' Touring Club, such was the relative importance of the two clubs.[6] But the cyclists, drawing a distinction between amateur cyclists and automobilists, directed the club's interest instead towards the RIA.

The secretary of the RIA was William Rees Jeffreys, who had previously represented the Cyclists' Touring Club on the RIA's council. In 1903 Rees Jeffreys left his position in the civil service at the Board of Trade and became the first administrative secretary of the Automobile Club.[7]

Rees Jeffreys was a pivotal figure in the early years of the road lobby. The Automobile Club was an exclusive all-male club, based in London's west end. As motoring spread, the Automobile Club set up a new organisation, the Motor Union, in 1903 to cater for the car's growing popularity and to keep its club exclusive. Rees Jeffreys was the first secretary of the Motor Union. He was also first secretary of another offshoot of the Automobile Club, the Commercial Motor Users' Association, which was set up in 1903 to represent bus and lorry operators. Three years later, in 1906, he went on to found the Motor Union Insurance Company and the Institution of Automobile Engineers.[8]

Rees Jeffreys used his contacts among motorists to increase their representation on the RIA, and correspondingly to diminish the influence of cyclists. Two of the new council members recruited by Rees Jeffreys were Conservative MPs, Sir Arthur Stanley, who was later chairman of the RAC, and John Scott Montagu, later Lord Montagu of Beaulieu.[9]

At the time the Cyclists' Touring Club was still the RIA's most important backer. In addition to its own contributions it raised money from individual cyclists by mailing out RIA subscription forms. But the cyclists were ceasing to regard cars and lorries as friends and more as a threat to their safe enjoyment of the public highway. In 1909 one member protested to the Cyclists' Touring Club about the practice of sending out RIA subscription forms on the 'ground that the motor industry had called it into existence'.[10] The protests had their effect and the club stopped sending out the forms.

Despite this setback the RIA waxed stronger. By 1914 its income was nearly £1,600,[11] which is equivalent to about £90,000 at today's prices. Although it had more than 330 individual members, largely a

2 *William Rees Jeffreys, the main force behind
the RIA, as he appeared to* The Bystander
in 1907

legacy of the Cyclists' Touring Club's efforts, the real power now lay
with its corporate members.

The SMMT was another offshoot of the Automobile Club, set up
in 1901 to separate the gentlemen motorists from the factory owners.
In 1905, the AA had been set up to frustrate police speed traps. The
AA employed scouts (on bicycles) to warn motorists of a speed trap
ahead.

By 1914 the four biggest contributors to the RIA were the AA, the
RAC, the SMMT and the London General Omnibus Company.[12]
Seventy years later the first three are still among the biggest backers
of today's equivalent of the RIA – the British Road Federation.

In these years before the First World War the RIA was at the peak
of its influence. The number of cars on the road was increasing
rapidly, doubling between 1904 and 1905, and then doubling again
by 1907. By the outbreak of war in 1914 there were sixteen times as
many cars as there had been in 1904.[13]

SOUTHERN PUBLISHING COMPANY

MEN OF ENGLAND

YOUR BIRTHRIGHT IS BEING TAKEN FROM YOU BY

RECKLESS MOTOR DRIVERS

Reckless Motorists drive over and kill your children.

Reckless Motorists drive over and kill both men and women.

Reckless Motorists kill your dogs.

Reckless Motorists kill your chickens.

Motorists fill your houses with dust.

Motorists spoil your clothes with dust.

Motorists, with dust and stink, poison the air we breathe, thus injuring your health

RECKLESS MOTORISTS have compelled one hundred thousand people to withdraw their horses and carriages from the public roads. It is estimated that one hundred thousand men have been thrown out of employment in consequence. It is estimated that five hundred thousand cyclists have been compelled to give up cycling through the Reckless Driving of Motorists. You cannot ride drive or walk on the public roads without the danger of being killed by Reckless Motorists.

MEN OF ENGLAND

Will you stand this tyranny any longer? Rise up, join together and bring pressure upon your representatives in Parliament and otherwise make it unpleasant and costly to the tyrants who endanger your lives and the lives of your dear ones. The Government refuse to protect you? Do not remain like tame sheep any longer, but act at once; then, and then only will your rights be restored to you.

3 *Early resistance to the road lobby, probably from the horse and cart lobby*

The motoring classes, lording it over humbler people just like Mr Toad, were the object of considerable resentment. Public attention focused on two problems: road safety and dust. The motoring clubs succeeded in raising the national speed limit from 12 mph to 20 mph in 1903, although not without opposition, both from those who thought the higher speed unsafe and those who wanted still higher speeds. The clubs also fought off an attempt to introduce driving tests.

Dust was a much greater problem with motor cars than it had been with bicycles. The railways regarded motor transport as a curiosity, a trifle to be experimented with. The railway lobby, which was anyway on the wane in Parliament, seems to have taken little interest in roads or their potential. There was some opposition to motor transport from people with an interest in horses, such as livery stables, but it was very patchy. And opponents of the motor vehicle could scarcely argue against measures which would solve the dust problem.

So the RIA was operating in a political vacuum. It offered a seductive policy, a technical fix, of the kind which has attracted governments ever since. Solving the problem of dust, by improving road surfaces, meant that the government avoided having to confront the issues raised by the spread of the motor car.

The cornerstone of Rees Jeffreys approach was to improve the system of administration.[14] He wanted county surveyors to be responsible for all roads in their area. He asked the County Surveyors' Society to join the RIA in a deputation to the government. The surveyors refused.[15]

So the RIA went to see the government on its own, in 1901. After twelve months of inaction, and fortified by supportive editorials in *The Times* and the *Daily Chronicle*, Rees Jeffreys wrote to the Prime Minister, suggesting an inquiry, which was set up in 1903.[16]

The committee was dominated by the RIA. Both Montagu and Stanley were members. The first witness was Rees Jeffreys, who was invited to join the committee after giving evidence. The County Surveyors' Society was miffed over Rees Jeffreys' influence. The secretary pointed out that 'his views are as nearly as possible identical with our own'.[17] But the Shropshire surveyor protested: 'I think we ought to resent a self-formed association like that endeavouring to teach us what we already know.'[18] It was just one of a series of internecine disputes that Rees Jeffreys became involved in.

The committee recommended setting up a national board to look after the roads, building bypasses to speed traffic round towns and creating powers for the compulsory purchase of land.

Outside its political lobbying, the RIA promoted technical developments. The surveyors could not agree on the best way to make roads, so as to minimise dust. Around 1907, the RIA held a series of trials which proved that tar was more effective than water at laying dust.[19]

In October 1908, the RIA organised the first international road congress in Paris. The treasurer of Rees Jeffreys' Motor Union argued that 'licensing fees . . . should be utilised for improving roadways'.[20] David Lloyd George, the Liberal Chancellor of the Exchequer, discussed the proposals with a group of RAC MPs, and the RIA[21] and dusted off the recommendations of the 1903 committee.

In his 1909 budget, Lloyd George proposed setting up a road fund, which would be administered by a new central authority. The revenue for the fund was to be raised by taxes on vehicles and petrol. The money would be spent on roads. The Roads Board was set up in 1910. It had the power to maintain roads or build new ones. It could also make grants to county councils to help them build roads.

The influence of the road lobby on the composition of the board was quite clear. Two of the board's five members represented the motoring organisations. The secretary was Rees Jeffreys, who resigned from his various posts in the road lobby. The only other full-time member of staff was Colonel Crompton, the vice-chairman of the RIA.

In only ten years the road lobby had achieved all its demands, and more. The board had a secure and growing source of income. It was not answerable to Parliament. And the road lobby was in a position to dominate the board.

The road lobby also had a firm friend in Lloyd George. He agreed to speak, for instance, at a road congress held in London in 1913. The congress seems to have been jointly organised by the Roads Board and the RIA. There was a last minute rush for tickets to hear the chancellor speak, and fearing a demonstration by suffragettes, the organisers banned all women from the meeting.[22]

The Roads Board was a failure, which was remarkable given its unparalleled powers. Rees Jeffreys, writing more than thirty years later, blamed the board's failings on political opposition, principally from the Treasury, landowners and the railways, and especially the antipathy of the chairman, Sir George Gibb, who was a railway director. But the truth was more prosaic. The board's administration was chaotic. It met forty-one times in nine years, including meetings which were attended only by the chairman. A civil service commission which investigated the board blamed both Gibb and Rees Jeffreys.[23]

Part of the problem was that Rees Jeffreys, as subsequent events proved, was not an easy person to get on with. Another problem was that Crompton, the board's consulting engineer, was not a road maker. The County Surveyors' Society sent a deputation to see Gibb and Rees Jeffreys in 1912 to complain, but left unsatisfied.[24] The board did not appoint a full-time chief engineer, Henry Maybury, Kent's county surveyor, until the end of 1913.[25] War followed a few months later.

The board could not spend all the money it received. In 1915 it spent only one-third of its income. Not surprisingly the Treasury diverted some of the motoring taxes to finance the war.[26] The road lobby, mostly through inexperience, had fluffed its chance. Rees Jeffreys resigned at the end of 1918. The board collapsed in internal wrangling and its functions were taken over by the Ministry of Transport. Maybury became the first director general of roads.

The immediate effect of Rees Jeffreys' appointment as secretary of the Roads Board was to cause a realignment of the road lobby. He resigned as secretary of the Motor Union which, now its prime mover was out of the way, promptly joined the AA.[27]

Meanwhile the RIA continued to be the focus for much political lobbying. The commercial vehicle users were an important influence on the RIA in the years immediately before the First World War. Not only was the London General Bus Company an important member, but its treasurer, Edward Shrapnell-Smith, was also secretary of the Commercial Motor Users' Association. During this period, the RIA opposed plans to charge tolls for buses on a new road in London and thwarted an attempt to lay new tram lines on another.[28]

Towards the end of the war, the road lobby split. The RIA ceased to be an umbrella group for all the road lobby. The first signs of a split came in 1916, when the SMMT slashed its support for the RIA by 75 per cent.[29]

The war caused problems for all groups in the road lobby. Many motorists were at the front, instead of motoring (although a substantial number did still drive, much to the fury of the popular press), and car sales dropped.

In 1917, the AA left the RIA, and was followed by the SMMT.[30] No love was lost between the AA and the RAC, which was still smarting over the defection of the Motor Union, and in 1919 the AA and the SMMT, contributing £1,000 each, set up their own lobby, the Motor Legislation Committee.[31] The RAC continued to finance the RIA, starting a schism which lasted into the 1950s. Not all links between the two groups were broken. Rees Jeffreys, who became chairman of the RIA on leaving the Roads Board, was vice-chairman of the Motor Legislation Committee until 1929.

The two groups had largely different areas of activity. The RIA was concerned with road building, and issues such as the removal of blind corners. The Motor Legislation Committee was dedicated to opposing further restrictions on motoring and abolishing the 20 mph speed limit.

The end of the Great War brought the road lobby into conflict with the railways for the first time. The reason was partly economic. Technical improvements to motor vehicles during the war had made the bus and lorry serious competitors for the railways. In addition the large number of vehicles coming on to the market, as war surplus, and often being sold to members of the armed forces returning home with their pay-offs, provided a cheap way of setting up a bus company or a haulage firm.

The first big battle was over the Ministry of Transport. Lloyd George, then Prime Minister, wanted to nationalise the railways and he wanted the ministry to control both railways and roads. It was this prospect which had prompted the AA and the SMTT to set up the Motor Legislation Committee.

In the debate on the bill the committee's chairman, William Joynson-Hicks MP, said that 280 MPs had just formed a committee to promote roads and they were all 'gravely suspicious of the roads being put under railway control'.[32] In the face of this opposition the government climbed down and amended its legislation. The railways were not nationalised. The main purposes of this new ministry, as a permanent secretary later put it, were:

> the emergence of motor vehicles as a major factor in the movement of passengers and goods, partly to supervise a large new road building programme (which did not in fact develop on anything like the scale originally envisaged), and partly to deal with the amalgamation of the railway companies.[33]

From this beginning the ministry's main concerns rapidly became the same as the road lobby's, although the ministry did not always share the same perspective. The amalgamation of the railways into four companies was over by 1923. The ministry could now concentrate on roads and motor vehicles.

Maybury, the new director general of roads, was the highest paid civil servant in the ministry, earning even more than the permanent secretary who was nominally his boss. At a special meeting of the County Surveyors' Society in November 1919, Maybury outlined his plans to his former colleagues for 5,000 miles of 'superclass' roads.[34]

But Maybury's plans depended on the road fund. And the road lobby was not the only one with its eyes on the fund. The basic problem remained the same. Money came into the fund faster than it went out. It was not helped by the administrative changes, nor by the relative weakness of the ministry, which was nearly abolished in the mid-1920s. By 1926 the road fund had accumulated £19 million.[35]

The Chancellor of the Exchequer, Winston Churchill, decided that the money would be better off in the Treasury than in the ministry's bank account. He laid plans to 'raid' the fund.

The road lobby got wind of Churchill's intentions, and organised a meeting at the RAC, chaired by Sir Arthur Stanley.[36] But the road lobby was divided, as the SMMT lamented.[37] Shrapnell-Smith, the secretary of the Commercial Motor Users Association recalled:

> Each section had its own plan. Unity of purpose was not achieved. The combined strength was thrown away, and this failure to work closely together on such a vital occasion subsequently proved highly prejudicial to the motoring community in negotiations with successive governments.[38]

Churchill raided the road fund in 1926, and again in 1927. The RIA did its best to stop further raids. It circulated Conservative constituency parties in 1927 to try to foment dissent on the government's backbenches. In 1928 the RIA sought support from traditional Conservative supporters, such as chambers of commerce. As a result hundreds of local authorities passed resolutions appealing to the government to save the fund.[39]

Road safety was the most contentious issue of the decade. Towards the end of the 1920s more than 6,000 people, half of them pedestrians, were being killed on the roads each year. The railways, too, were increasingly concerned about the competition from buses and lorries for passengers and freight.

The government responded in 1928 by setting up a Royal Commission on Transport. In 1929 the Pedestrians' Association was founded. It was a counterbalance to the influence of the Motor Legislation Committee. Just as the Motor Legislation Committee wanted motoring freed of its fetters, the Pedestrians wanted it more closely controlled. But they were on their own in this fight because the cyclists were still tied up with the RIA.

In 1929 Lord Cecil, the Pedestrians' Association president, introduced a bill in Parliament designed to improve road safety. Its main measure was the introduction of driving tests. The road lobby was horrified. Cecil withdrew the bill, in favour of government legislation, based on the report of the Royal Commission.[40]

In May 1930, the government sponsored National Safety Week. Pedestrians and the cyclists had a place on the organising committee, but it was dominated by the road lobby, the AA, the Commercial Motor Users' Association, the RAC, the RIA and the SMMT. The railway and tramway associations refused to have anything to do with the propaganda week, and no attempt was made to persuade them otherwise. However, considerable attempts were made to persuade another group, the Boy Scouts, that refused, to change their mind.[41]

The cost of the week was paid for by the RAC, the SMMT, omnibus owners, the Motor Agents' Association and the National Safety First Association – now the Royal Society for the Prevention of Accidents. Apart from a broadcast by a vaudeville artist called Stainless Stephen, the tone of the propaganda was that the onus was on pedestrians to avoid accidents. The RIA, in a wireless broadcast, warned children of 'the risks of carelessness when crossing or playing in the street'.[42] By the end of the year, 7,300 people were dead, half of them pedestrians, a sharp increase over previous years.

The National Safety First Association had a curious outlook on road safety. It was partly financed by the SMMT. In 1928 it produced a chart showing that 64 per cent of accidents could not be avoided by drivers. It included such categories as skidding on tramlines (2 per cent) and where the pedestrian crossing the road was infirm.[43]

The government's legislation, which became the 1930 Road Traffic Act, was scarcely likely to please the pedestrians. It abolished the 20 mph speed limit, and put nothing in its place. It did, however, introduce compulsory third party insurance (after all, someone has to pay the undertakers). It also went some way to appeasing the railways by introducing bus licensing.

Road deaths remained alarmingly high, reaching a peak in 1934. The public outcry forced the government to retreat. The 1934 Road Traffic Act reintroduced a speed limit – of 30 mph in built up areas – and brought in driving tests. In a vain attempt to stave off speed limits, the Motor Legislation Committee gave the National Safety First Association £1,000 to assist it in its campaign against the limits.[44]

Meanwhile out of the public eye the RIA's efforts were meeting with more success. By 1929 its income had reached £3,600 – about £115,000 at today's prices.[45] It set up a parliamentary committee, with some sixty members, which had Lloyd George as its vice-chairman. It continued to push a more centralised highway administration and had its success with the 1929 Local Government Act, which made county councils responsible for all roads, outside the major urban areas. The RIA called it 'a valuable improvement' and called for a £100 million spending programme 'to modernise our highway system'.[46]

It distributed a pamphlet during 1929, a general election year, with the tortuous title 'Roads. The dependence of industrial prosperity and social progress upon systematic road development' in support of its programme. More than 50,000 copies were distributed to local authorities, MPs and the usual round of chambers of commerce and rotary clubs.[47] Rees Jeffreys, accompanied by Mervyn O'Gorman from the RAC, led a deputation to see the First Labour Minister of Transport, Herbert Morrison. Morrison promised 'there must be a big push in connection with road development'. He instituted a system of government grants for local council road building, a 75 per cent grant for major roads and 60 per cent for secondary roads.[48] The system lasted until 1974.

The RIA had also taken the lead in calling for more research into roads, ever since its tar trials. The RIA and the County Surveyors' Society continued to push for a central research bureau. The Road Research Board (later the Road Research Laboratory) was set up in 1933. One of the board's members was O'Gorman, the RAC representative on the RIA.

Cyclists were becoming increasingly unhappy at the activities of the RIA. But the Cyclists' Touring Club, still an important political force, was controlled by an old guard. They still thought the motorist a friend, even though in the early 1930s the club was inundated with claims for legal assistance from cyclists who had been involved in accidents with motor vehicles.

In 1931 the club's representative on the RIA was made a vice-chairman of the association in an attempt to placate the restive cyclists. He reported back to the club, at unusual length, 'the interests of cyclists . . . have at all times been adequately voiced at its meetings'.[49] He died in 1932. In 1933 the club decided to resign, on an 18 to 4 vote.[50]

The dispute spilled over into the columns of the club's magazine. Colonel C. H. L. Baskerville, who had represented the club on the RIA since before the First World War, regretted the decision. Chas Hopkinson did not. He said the change had come twenty years too late, continuing prophetically:

With every road widened and cemented, wire fencing in place of hedges, and everything done to move a maximum mileage in a minimum time at minimum cost the whole policy is anathema to the tourist out for scenery, quietude and rural simplicity. The commercial transport interest will never rest content until the countryside is scarred with cement tracks, and every secondary road is turned into a trunk road.[51]

The loss of the Cyclists' Touring Club's £25 subscription was scarcely a crippling blow to the RIA. Neither was it an important political loss. Baskerville, and others of the old guard, continued to represent 'cyclists' on the RIA.[52] Politically, too, the RIA had made an important gain in the shape of the Transport and General Workers' Union, which joined in 1929. Its first representative was Ernest Bevin, who in 1933 lent his support to an RIA plan for a new road from London to South Wales. The RIA exhibited the plan at the *Daily Mail*'s Ideal Home Exhibition.[53]

The Royal Commission on Transport's final report, which was published in 1931, recommended licensing road hauliers. The Commercial Motor Users' Association representative on the commission wrote a minority report, dissenting.

The railway companies returned to the attack in 1932, telling the incoming Conservative transport minister, Percy Pybus, that speed limits and maximum weight for lorries were being widely ignored. The complaints have an all too modern ring. Pybus told the cabinet: 'there is undoubtedly much ground in this complaint'.[54]

Pybus was caught between two powerful forces. Although the railways' power was declining, they could still make their influence felt. He could also not afford to offend the road lobby. Speaking at the Commercial Motor Users' Association's lunch in February 1932, he promised lorry operators they would be consulted. 'The department has always consulted representative bodies.'[55]

Pybus's solution was to set up an inquiry, and balance the four representatives from the railways with four from the roads. He refused to have a representative from the Pedestrians' Association, even though safety was an important part of the railways' case. The inquiry was chaired by Sir Arthur Salter.

One county surveyor told the inquiry of lorries being two or three tons over the limit, or vehicles making lengthy detours to avoid checks, of firms sending scouts ahead to check for constables and of two lorries starting out legally loaded passing the check point, and then amalgamating their loads with the empty one returning to base.[56]

The magazine *Commercial Motor* complained: 'haulage interests have to a great extent being outmanoeuvred . . . long distance haulage is in the position of a criminal in the dock',[57] which if the county surveyor was right was exactly where it should have been. The Salter Committee recommended the licensing of goods vehicles and heavier taxation. The 1933 Road and Rail Act introduced licensing for goods vehicles.

In the 1920s the road lobby had been weakened by its internal divisions. The Salter inquiry was the stimulus which united the lobby.

Faced with this assault by the railways some of the main groups in the lobby, including the AA, the commercial motor users, the SMMT and the RAC, held a conference, again chaired by Arthur Stanley, to discuss their reactions.[58] The conference met again in September, and this time the meeting included wider interests, such as the Asphalt Roads Association and the RIA, and agreed to conduct a joint campaign.

The chief organiser was Frank Pick, a director of the London General, although Rees Jeffreys characteristically also laid claim to this role.[59] Pick had a long, and largely unnoticed association with the road lobby. He set up one lobby grouping in 1912[60] and for much of the 1920s was active with both the Commercial Motor Users' Association and the RIA.

Speaking at the House of Commons at the end of 1933, Pick said that the Salter report was 'the fruit of railway propaganda'. He said that the report (which had concluded that lorries did not pay for the damage they did to roads) put too high a figure on road spending and accused the railways 'of keeping open many small uneconomic lines which ought to be out of commission'.[61]

In private, Pick was working hard to unite the road interests against what he saw as the common enemy. The problem was that some lorry operators thought they could gain out of a licensing system, while others felt threatened by it. 'I almost despair of getting road transport to adopt a common policy. We seem to split badly over the question of licensing. . . . I often wonder . . . how we shall succeed in presenting a united front.'[62]

Out of this conference of motor organisation came the BRF, which was established as a separate pressure group towards the end of 1932. The Commercial Motor Users' Association and the SMMT were among the founder members. The first chairman was Frank Pick.

From the outset the BRF was intended to have a wider role than just fighting goods vehicle licensing. It was also going to press for more roads. However, there was a tacit understanding that it would pursue this campaign through the RIA. The SMMT rapidly concluded that the BRF could press for road building on its own, and that it did not need the RIA, or Rees Jeffreys.

At the beginning of 1933 Rees Jeffreys wrote a long and pained letter to Pick. He said that the SMMT had assured him when the BRF was set up that there would be no overlap between the BRF and the RIA, and that the BRF would 'conduct its road propaganda through the RIA'.

He went on to suggest that the BRF should make an agreed

contribution to the funds of the RIA . . . in view of the vital
importance of road maintenance and development to the
supporters of the federation it is submitted that the contribution
from the federation should be a really substantial one.[63]

He stood no chance of success. The BRF had not only usurped the
RIA's political role, but it was also taking away the RIA's financial
support. By 1933 the RIA's income had dropped below £1,000, and
it continued to fall throughout the 1930s. In 1935 Rees Jeffreys
asked the SMMT for £250. He was told that an 'application for a
subscription would be unlikely to be successful'.[64] At this time the
BRF had an annual income of around £10,000.[65]

Pick's activities clearly irked the ministry. In May 1933, he was
appointed vice-chairman of the newly nationalised London Transport.
One of the conditions of his appointment, underlined by hand on the
ministry's copy is: 'you would not accept any other paid directorships
or engage in any work which would conflict with the duties of your
position as a member of the board'.[66] He subsequently said he had
been told to stop his political activities.[67] He resigned from the BRF.

Of the three umbrella groups, the Motor Legislation Committee
was wound up in 1943, and the RIA ceased to have any political
importance after the war. In 1949 the AA could write that relations
with the RIA 'although outwardly cordial, are somewhat difficult to
define'.[68] Even the BRF hibernated during the war, and it was run by
a caretaker. Rees Jeffreys was prompted to remark: 'The BRF has
never taken root and cannot be expected to do so for obvious reasons.'
The SMMT's secretary retorted: 'I do not necessarily share your fears
regarding the future of the BRF, but that is probably a matter of
opinion.'[69]

Despite the RIA's loss of power it had achieved one fundamental
change. It established the philosophy that the roads should be made
to suit the traffic. Before the RIA no single philosophy prevailed. At
times, such as the days when wagons were compelled to have wide
wheels, so as to roll the roads, instead of breaking them up, the theory
that held sway was that the traffic should be made to suit the roads.
The RIA changed all that. As Beatrice and Sidney Webb, keen advocates of better roads, put it: 'the roads have once more got to be
made to accommodate the traffic, not the traffic constrained to suit
the roads'.[70] The RIA changed that. And the philosophy that roads
should be made to suit the traffic ruled for the next sixty years.

4 One thousand miles of motorways

In the summer of 1943, fifteen years before the first motorway was opened, a crucial meeting was held in London. This meeting, which was held in an elegant Georgian house overlooking Bloomsbury Square – in the days before it was desecrated by an underground car park – effectively determined Britain's motorway policy until the 1970s.

The meeting was chaired by the SMMT's secretary, Colonel D. McLagen. It was formally a meeting of the BRF's publicity committee. But the guise is deceptive. Also at the meeting were five people who did not normally attend the BRF's publicity committee. One was Arthur Floyd, the secretary of the County Surveyors' Society. Also sitting at the table was Rees Jeffreys, who was representing the RAC, as well as people from the Institution of Highway Engineers, the Institution of Municipal and County Engineers and the Royal Institute of British Architects.[1]

This meeting decided to adopt the County Surveyors' Society's plan for 1,000 miles of motorways, or motor roads as they were then known. This target was approved by the government, and pursued by the lobby consistently until the roads were completed in 1971. The meeting's achievement was that it unified the factions in the road lobby about one target, shelving the aspirations of the highway engineers and the RAC for larger networks.[2]

The idea of building motorways dates back until at least 1903.[3] But an attempt to legislate for roads that could be used only by motor traffic failed in 1909. The AA and the RAC opposed the idea, because they feared that cars would be restricted to these roads.[4]

The counties had become responsible for main roads in 1929. But the next logical step, of the state taking over the main roads, which would make building new motorways administratively easier, caused a furious row in the road lobby.

The BRF and the SMMT called for a 'central highway authority'.[5] However, the county surveyors were naturally reluctant to give up

4 Alfred Barnes,
  Minister of Transport, 1945–51

5 Ernest Marples,
  Minister of Transport, 1959–64

6 Barbara Castle,
  Minister of Transport, 1965–8

7 *One thousand miles of motorway came from this unpretentious house, at 21 Southampton Place*

their newly acquired power.[6] They were backed by Rees Jeffreys, who was annoyed because the BRF was increasingly supplanting his RIA.

The SMMT sent the government a memorandum in 1935, arguing privately 'we will see no progress on main roads at all until a central authority is able to view them from start to finish'.[7] While the BRF wanted a board controlled by the road lobby, 'interests which do not contribute . . . should be without representation'.[8]

The RIA's propaganda committee, which was chaired by a former chief roads engineer at the Ministry of Transport,[9] came out in support of a central authority. Rees Jeffreys fired off an angry note telling the committee it had gone beyond its brief which was 'propaganda not policy'.[10]

To the SMMT he fired off an even more intemperate letter: 'For a committee of motor manufacturers and traders to sit down and formulate a road policy is equivalent to a committee of road surveyors sitting down to design a motor car.'[11] The RIA produced a more veiled rejection: 'There is a demand in certain quarters for the creation of a national central highways department . . . the association feels there are simpler methods.'[12]

Rees Jeffreys' reaction was one of pure pique. Earlier the same year he had argued that 'the time is now ripe for . . . a central commission to plan . . . new roads and bridges of the kind that is demanded by through motor traffic'.[13] He pushed his point home over lunch with the Minister of Transport, Leslie Hore-Belisha.[14]

The road lobby pushed home its case during the 1935 general election.[15] The government promised a £100 million spending programme. After winning the election, the government set about redeeming its pledge. The first step was administrative, which had the virtue, for the government, of avoiding having to put its money where its mouth was. Under the 1936 Trunk Roads Act the government took over 4,500 miles of roads, in a move which *The Times* described as 'nationalising' British roads.[16] The British Road Tar Association took the opportunity to call for a coronation road plan, to celebrate the crowning of King Edward VIII.

The road lobby was increasingly looking towards the German autobahns for its inspiration. In 1934 the international road congress was held in Munich. The Asphalt Roads Association reported that 'good speed surfaces are considered essential' and a 'preliminary towards the organisation of motor car manufacturing as the key industry of the new Germany'.[17]

In May 1937 the AA enrolled a new member. It was proposed by the chairman, seconded by the vice-chairman, and unanimously agreed that His Excellency Joachim von Ribbentrop the German ambassador be elected an honorary member of the association.[18]

Both von Ribbentrop and the AA's secretary, Stenson Cooke, were former wine salesmen.

The formal handover of trunk roads to the Ministry of Transport took place on 1 April. A few weeks later, the ministry received an invitation from Roger Gresham Cooke, the BRF's secretary, to take part in a German Roads Delegation, the result of the contact between the AA and von Ribbentrop.[19]

Gresham Cook said that the general inspector of German highways, Doctor Fritz Todt, had invited a party of about 200 people to inspect the German road system. 'Any officer accepting the invitation will be put to no expense' he wrote. The ministry declined to take part in the delegation. Stenson Cooke wrote back, on behalf of the delegation, that he was disappointed 'that the party will not include some of our good friends from the Ministry of Transport'.[20]

Eventually a group of 255 people, including fifty-eight members of parliament, fifty-four county surveyors and other councillors and road engineers left these shores on 24 September 1937, to inspect the

8 *The English road builders get to know Adolf Hitler's roads – how the Nazi press viewed the German Roads Delegation,* Illustrierter Beobachter, 14 October 1937

autobahns of the Third Reich. The visit was a typical public relations exercise, with the emphasis on conviviality.

A typical day's programme was to spend the morning driving round Munich, followed by lunch at the Preysing Palais and then a visit to 'the world famous Oktoberfest'. The delegates were provided with an 'ample supply of printed notes' just in case their memories failed'.[21]

For the Third Reich, which financed much of the expedition, the delegation was a propaganda coup. Doctor Todt who was the equivalent of Minister of Transport, accompanied the delegates on part of their tour, and gave a state reception in their honour. He laid on a special train for them to witness the meeting of Herr Hitler and Signor Mussolini, in Berlin's Olympic Stadium.[22] One county surveyor reported: 'needless to say there was a large response to this additional item'.

Back in Britain the delegation produced its official report: 'we recommend that the principle of the motorway system be adopted in Britain'.[23] The reports from individual county surveyors began to flood into the ministry, all couched in strikingly similar terms, as part of a clearly coordinated campaign.

The ministry remained sceptical. The delegates were impressed 'by the greatness of the task which had been undertaken by the Germans . . . the magnitude and cost of these great works appear to have presented no obstacle', although the report concedes that the traffic was 'thin'.[24] The minister, Leslie Burgin, commented tersely: 'I know of no comparable instance in road making when a road has been designed and built utterly regardless of the volume of traffic which it bears.'[25]

One county surveyor described compulsory purchase in Germany:

> Land is acquired by purchase in the usual way and if the proprietors refuse to sell the company (the subsidiary of the German state railways which built the autobahns) has the right of expropriation . . . the inspector general (Todt) is the deciding authority in the process of expropriation and exchange of land.[26]

The delegation's report says 'it transpired that 98 per cent of the farmers voluntarily agreed to a sale'. Burgin remarked: 'one may well ask what meaning can be attached to the word voluntarily in a totalitarian state'.[27]

The engineers in the ministry generally favoured widening existing roads, rather than building motorways. And the ministry's administrators were suspicious about the vested interests involved in the delegation. 'Practically all persons have a strong road bias', wrote one civil servant, pointing out that the German roads had an obvious military purpose. Another minutes that 'the advocates [of motor roads] are primarily persons interested in the promotion of transport by road and include some of the interests who would be financially benefited if the proposal they advocate is adopted.'

Another civil servant minuted:

> The delegation shows the cloven hoof . . . when they point out that the motor industry is of immense importance. In view of the composition of the delegation it seems a sign of undue modesty not to have referred to the concrete industry.[28]

Later in 1937 Todt paid a visit to London where he was entertained by the delegation at a dinner, held in his honour at the Connaught Rooms. He attended the ninth Public Works Roads and Transport Conference, where he would doubtless have had a passing interest in a paper by an air ministry official – on air raid precautions.[29]

The German Roads Delegation, led by the AA, the BRF and the County Surveyors' Society, met Burgin in March 1938 to press their case for motorways. On the same day, Burgin also met the parliamentary road group. The minister's brief for the meeting contains a rare example of concern about the railways having an influence on road policy. The civil service advised Burgin to keep an 'open mind' and warned of the danger of diverting traffic from rail to road, because if the railways lost money they would have to be subsidised. 'If so on what industry is the burden of increased taxation most likely to fall? The question hardly calls for a reply.'[30]

But Burgin was coming round to the idea of motorways. He told the delegation that he would 'explore the reaction in high places to the desirability of building an experimental length of motor road'. Shortly before this meeting, Lancashire County Council had submitted a proposal for a motorway, running north to south through the county. The Cabinet subsequently discussed the scheme, but the Treasury opposed it. After a meeting between Burgin and the Chancellor of the Exchequer, Sir John Simon, in July, the plan was dropped.[31] And the BRF's call for money to be switched from the defence fund into road building was not heeded.[32]

As war approached, the German connection became more obviously sensitive. The AA had already been forced to deny that the delegation's visit was designed to support the German regime.[33] So the German Roads Delegation was transmuted into the Modern Roads Movement. Its most noteworthy aspect is some remarkably expensive notepaper, which was presumably junked at the onset of war.

The county surveyors continued working on their plans for a 1,000-mile network of motorways. Their society presented its final plans to the ministry in May 1938. The plans were crudely drawn in crayon on a road map published by the magazine *Tit-Bits*, a publication best known for the scantily clad females that were strewn across its pages.[34]

The outbreak of war caused a hiatus in this lobbying. The country, and even the road lobby, had more important concerns than motorways. Little happened for three years.

In 1942, the County Surveyors Society set up a joint committee with the municipal engineers to draw up post-war road plans. This committee discussed technical details of the new roads, such as gradients, the radius of curves and the width of carriageways. In 1942, the county surveyors presented the ministry's chief engineer with a plan for a motorway from London to Birmingham.[35]

At the beginning of 1943, the county surveyors were looking around for allies. They had already had 'helpful talks' with A. Lyddon, the ministry's deputy chief engineer.[36] And Arthur Floyd, the county surveyors' secretary, could write:

> Personally I am in not the slightest doubt that if the municipal and county engineers, my own association and the two motor associations were to produce an agreed scheme it must inevitably prevail.[37]

In the mean time the RAC had produced plans for a 2,000-mile network of motorways, while the Institution of Highway Engineers wanted 3,000 miles.

The BRF had already publicly backed the *Tit-Bits* plan in a pamphlet sent to the government in 1942. Opinion in the ministry was beginning to swing towards motorways. Although an administrator could minute that the pamphlet 'seems to be a curious and indigestible mixture of truths, half truths and misstatements', Sir Frederick Cook, the chief roads engineer, wrote: 'it seems an interesting paper'.[38]

By the midsummer of 1943, opinion in the road lobby was beginning to coalesce around the *Tit-Bits* plan. McLagen wrote to Rees Jeffreys, as the RAC's representative:

> We have no quarrel with the ideas of other organisations who wish to go further, but what we do wish to avoid is an opposition or criticism from other bodies as to the extent of the motorways which we advocate.[39]

So agreement was quite easy to reach at that July meeting in Bloomsbury Square. Both of the groups which had supported larger mileages swung behind the county surveyors. The highway engineers

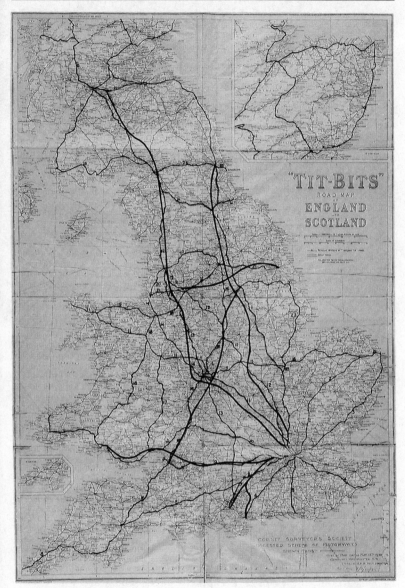

9 *The* Tit-Bits *motorway map*

promised 'all support' while Rees Jeffreys grudgingly approved 'it was the minimum needed'.[40]

Later that month, the BRF and the county surveyors achieved even broader support for the *Tit-Bits* plan at a meeting which included the AA, the RIA, the Institution of Civil Engineers, as well as the Royal

Society for the Prevention of Accidents, the Town and Country Planning Association and the Council for the Preservation of Rural England.[41]

The road lobby continued to press its plans on the government, which at the beginning of 1944 announced plans for a limited number of motor roads. When the BRF redrew the county surveyors' plans for public consumption, Lyddon, by now the ministry's chief roads engineer, minuted: 'The recommendations seem to me to be sound and reasonable.' The ministry opened a file called 'The Master Plan'.[42]

In May 1946, Alfred Barnes, the Minister of Transport in the new Labour government, announced a ten-year plan for building 800 miles of motorways, a network not much different from that proposed by the County Surveyors' Society. The plans, though no longer sketches on a *Tit-Bits* road map, were exhibited in the House of Commons' tea room.[43]

In July, the BRF, together with the Cement and Concrete Association, the RHA and the SMMT, formed a deputation to meet Barnes. The civil service briefed Barnes, 'the federation is an important body'. The meeting was remarkably chummy, given that the BRF and the RHA were actively organising a vitriolic campaign against the nationalisation of road haulage. The BRF's chairman told Barnes: 'Although inland transport can give rise to controversial political questions these need not touch road construction, which all members of my federation sincerely wish will never be a party issue.' He went on to offer the BRF's help with publicity and asked that it should be 'taken into the minister's confidence in order that the widespread facilities available to the federation may be used to the best advantage'.[44]

Barnes accepted the BRF's offer and was (understandably) 'particularly interested in what the federation does with regard to general press publicity'.[45] The onset of the post-war financial crisis meant that the road building plans had to be postponed.

Although building roads was out of the question, the government did go ahead with legislation enabling motorways to be built. The BRF sent out copies of a pamphlet called 'The Case for Motorways' to 35,000 people in 1948, in support of the Special Roads Bill.[46]

Barnes was duly grateful and in the November debate on the second reading of the bill said 'the BRF has provided a good deal of valuable publicity on this subject'. It was left to Hugh Molson, a Conservative MP who was one of the bill's few critics, to point out the unhealthy closeness that now existed between the road lobby and the ministry:

An important argument is put forward by the British Road
Federation, which we must assume is approved by the Minister
of Transport. It is perhaps unusual and unconventional for a
minister to cut short the exposition of his own bill and his
justification of it by referring to documents which have been
circulated by a private body. . . . [47]

But Molson was a lone voice. Peter Thorneycroft, who was also a
Conservative and a noted spokesman for motoring interests, even
proposed a clause that would make consulting the BRF compulsory.
Barnes baulked, but did give an assurance that the AA, the BRF
and the RAC would be consulted, as well as the British Transport
Commission, thus elevating the road lobby to the same rank and
status as the largest and most important nationalised industry that
Labour had created.[48]

Lack of money continued to be the road lobby's stumbling block.
Preparatory work on the Severn Bridge had to be stopped, and
although the BRF launched a campaign stressing the importance of a
link to South Wales, it had no effect.[49]

In 1949 the county surveyor of Lancashire, James Drake, a long-
standing motorway enthusiast, drew up revised plans for a north
south motorway through Lancashire. Part of it would become the
M6. Drake sent off his plan to the ministry. The BRF quickly
followed, with a delegation to see Barnes, in support of the plan. But
it was shelved. The Labour government never escaped its financial
problems.

The road lobby returned to the attack in 1952, in a final push to
get motorways built in Britain. It concentrated its effort in support
of Drake's plans. Within six years, Britain's first motorway had been
opened – in Lancashire.

Although the case is now more than thirty years old, it remains a
classic example of the road lobby at work. The technique has barely
changed in the intervening years. The road lobby first seeks the
support of third parties. Local commercial and trade bodies are a
good bet for the lobby, because they are full of ready-made allies
such as lorry operators and car dealers. Then these groups lobby the
government. Next the road lobby wheels in the local MPs, either
contacting them directly or through its new-found allies. Combined
with local press coverage, the civil service in far away London
becomes convinced that there is a problem, and also of the need to
solve it.

The campaign started in May 1952 when the Burnley Chamber of
Commerce passed a resolution in support of the north south

motorway, and sent it off to the ministry.[50] Ten days later Warrington's Chamber of Commerce followed suit: 'the attention of my council has been directed to the Lancashire road plan on which the British Road Federation have spent so much intensive thought'.[51]

At the beginning of July, Preston town council wrote to the ministry in support of the motorway. Then three MPs wrote in. One of them, Julian Amery, who was writing on behalf of the Preston town council, enclosed a speech by the BRF's vice-chairman, Christopher Brunner, on the need for the motorway. The ministry opened a new file on the road.[52]

At a meeting in Preston, James Drake described the road through the town as 'Britain's most dangerous road' and made the rather unlikely claim that a bypass could save 500 lives.[53]

In October, the BRF kept up the pressure by organising a conference on Lancashire roads. The three co-sponsors of this conference were the BRF, Lancashire County Council (Drake's employer), and the Lancashire and Merseyside Industrial Development Association. Drake was the main speaker, supported by Brunner.[54]

The three sponsors wrote to the ministry. The council also wrote separately to the Prime Minister and the Chancellor of the Exchequer, although this had little effect because the letters were simply redirected to the Ministry of Transport.[55]

Inside the ministry the civil service suggested 'raising Lancashire roads up the pecking order'.[56] Eleven Lancashire MPs set up a committee to study the Lancashire roads plan. On 18 December, the minister announced plans to build bypasses of Lancaster and Preston. (Plans for a small section of the M5 were also announced on the same day.)[57]

Still the road lobby kept up the pressure. A local MP writing to the minister early in 1954 was told by the minister that the Preston bypass might be advanced by one year.[58]

At the end of 1954, the Warrington Chamber of Commerce wrote to the new minister, John Boyd-Carpenter, 'members . . . have had extensive experience of motoring . . . they are unanimous . . . that there is no part of Britain . . . where the need for entirely new roads or for large-scale improvements is so desperate'. The effect of the letter was somewhat spoilt by the chamber's failure to discover the new minister's name.[59]

In July 1955, a group of Lancashire MPs went to see the minister to press for an early start on the Preston bypass. Boyd-Carpenter held out some hope. 'I am anxious that work should be started on the Preston bypass as soon as possible.'[60] Work did start on it in June

1956 – one year before work started on any other motorway in Lancashire.

The Preston bypass was opened in December 1958, and closed again within weeks as huge cracks appeared in its surface. When Harold Macmillan, the then Prime Minister, opened it, three motorways were under construction in Britain – two of them were in Lancashire.

Drake later wrote:

Many organisations and individuals have tried to further the construction of motorways in Britain and none more than the British Road Federation and the Roads Campaign Council, who have made unceasing efforts to draw attention to the essential role of motorways in the economic and social welfare of the nation.[61]

John Boyd-Carpenter, the minister at the time, recalled that in the mid-1950s 'public anger was rising against the inadequacies of our road system and the inaction of the government in respect of it. The road haulage industry and the AA and the RAC were conducting campaigns of agitation.'[62] But although the ministry's files are full of the road lobby's efforts, there is scant evidence of any public concern. The ministry's large file on the north south motorway has just two letters which appear to be from members of the public. Every other communication is from the road lobby, or one of its known and predictable allies.[63]

In February 1955 Boyd-Carpenter announced the first tranche of motorways, including the M1 and the M6, a road that would link Birmingham with Preston, or at least with the Preston bypass. It was the traditional pre-election sweetener. Two months later, the Roads Campaign Council launched its roads crusade, as it termed it, orchestrated by the right-wing group, Aims of Industry.

The council took a mobile film show around Britain, concentrating on sensitive marginal constituencies in the run up to the general election. 'Whichever way you look Britain's roads are in a jam', said one pamphlet, exhorting its readers to 'ask your MP what he is *doing* about it'.[64] The crusade continued into 1956 with the council pushing for a bridge across the Severn and the widening of the M1. A petition with 500,000 signatures on it was presented to Parliament.

In 1957 Harold Watkinson, the new Minister of Transport, announced a new boost for the road programme, with five new routes, including the M2, the M4 (and the Severn Bridge) and the M5. The programme was still based on the *Tit-Bits* plan, as modified in the House of Commons' tea room, with 800 miles of motorway. But by

1960 the ministry's road engineers and the road lobby was pushing for the target to be raised.[65]

After the general election of 1959, Ernest Marples became Minister of Transport. It was scarcely a set back for the road lobby. Marples was a road builder. He owned 64,000 out of the 80,000 shares in Marples Ridgeway, the civil engineering firm which specialised in roads.[66] This shareholding became a scandal in 1960 when the firm was successful in its bid to build the Hammersmith Flyover in London. For although it was a local council road, the ministry was heavily involved in local road planning, giving the road a 75 per cent grant.[67] Marples defended his continued shareholding by saying that he took no active part in the firm's affairs and that the sale of his shares had taken some time to arrange.[68] It was subsequently said that the shares were sold to his wife.[69]

In 1962, Marples upped the motorway target from 800 to 1,000 miles, and set a completion date of 1972.[70] But the road lobby was looking for a much more substantial increase in the target. In 1961, the County Surveyors' Society had set up a sub-committee to look at future motorway plans. The six-strong committee included such well-known motorway advocates as Drake and Stuart Maynard Lovell, the county surveyor of Yorkshire's West Riding.[71] The county surveyors sent off their plan to the ministry. But it met with a cool reception. Only an 'exceptionally cordial' meeting between the surveyors and the ministry's chief engineer in 1964 restored relations between the two.[72] The surveyors published their plan in 1968.

In 1965, as part of the pressure for a higher target, the Roads Campaign Council published its demands for £7 billion to be spent on roads. It commissioned a report from E. Victor Morgan, an economics professor at University College Cardiff, and a leading light in the Institute of Economic Affairs. Morgan wanted an additional 1,700 miles of motorway (based on the county surveyors' plans) as well as the widening of existing roads and a massive urban road building programme.[73]

In the meantime the road lobby set about accelerating the rate at which motorways were built. The National Economic Development Office set up a roads working party, which was fairly well-dominated by the road lobby. The chairman of the working party explained that building a road took seven years, of which five were spent arguing about it. He wanted to cut down the time for argument.[74]

Barbara Castle acted on this report, and introduced regional road construction units, staffed partly by the ministry and partly by engineers from the local county surveyors, to speed up road building. The first road construction unit was set up in the north-west. Its head was James Drake.

The new system certainly did speed up motorway building. The first 500 miles took nearly ten years to build. The second 500 miles were built in just four years. The 1,000-mile target was completed slightly ahead of schedule.

> Long promised for completion by the end of 1972 this 1,000 miles came . . . ahead of schedule, and much of the credit is due to the federation for maintaining the emphasis on completion with a firm target date.[75]

In 1969, the government published a green paper on the future of the road programme. It was pushed through cabinet with barely any discussion.[76] It showed the first 1,000 miles of motorway and then proposed building another 1,000 miles. The network 'bore a close resemblance' to the county surveyors' plan.[77]

The scene now shifts a couple of miles across London to another elegant Georgian house, this time overlooking Manchester Square. The road lobby was meeting again to discuss the future motorway plan.

Eight men sat around that table in April 1971. There was Robert Phillipson, the BRF's director, who chaired the meeting, and his deputy, Ken Cannell. Tony Lee was there from the RAC, Basil Rogers from the AA, Frank Lyon from the RHA, John Guttridge from the FTA, as well as two others. The aim of the meeting was simple: to set a new target for the motorway builders.

They discussed two options: a 3,000-mile target and a 4,000-mile target. They settled for 3,000 miles, on the grounds that 4,000 miles would take longer to build and a target date of 1984 would not be a good image for their public relations.[78]

Two months later, Peter Walker, the Secretary of State for the Environment, whose brief included transport, announced the new target. He envisaged an eventual network of 3,500 miles of new roads. Two thousand miles would be motorways, the rest dual carriageways. It was near enough for the road lobby.[79]

10 *Bill Rodgers, Secretary of*
State for Transport, 1976–9

11 *Nicholas Ridley, Secretary of*
State for Transport 1983–6

5 Bulldozing London

Now is the time to get the bulldozers to work.
Because even if a fleet of bulldozers was turned
loose in London and all the drivers were blindfolded
they could not do much unnecessary work because
of the immensity of the problem.[1]

To Colonel Stuart Maynard Lovell, the county surveyor of Yorkshire's West Riding, London was an obstacle for drivers, one that should be bulldozed out of the way. It has so far largely escaped. But other towns have not been so lucky, including the main town of the old West Riding – Leeds. Indeed Leeds was so proud of its achievements that the Post Office used to frank mail 'Leeds. Motorway city of the seventies' – a habit that continued well into the 1980s.

The key to the road lobby basic aims, of boosting car sales and road building, was the cities. In Britain four out of ten people live in eight urban areas. If motorists remained bottled up in city traffic jams, the road lobby would continue to fall short of its sales targets.

In the mid-1950s, the road lobby switched its attention from national motorways to urban road building. As the BRF put it: 'with the need for intercity motorways largely accepted the federation . . . continued its work to secure public acceptance of the principle of carrying such motorways into and through the cities they are designed to serve'.[2]

The push for urban motorways began in 1955. The BRF exhibited a working model at the motor show and the London *Evening Standard* (with 'considerable assistance' from the BRF) mounted a campaign to 'build better roads now'.[3]

In 1956, two years before the country's first motorway of any sort opened, the BRF held a conference on urban motorways. Two top civil servants, Allan Baker, the ministry's chief engineer, and William Glanville, the head of the government's Road Research Laboratory, told the conference: 'a comprehensive solution must include new

12 'No single road development scheme could make a greater contribution to the relief of growing traffic congestion' – John Boyd-
Carpenter, in 1954, on turning London's Park Lane into a dual
carriageway

roads and . . . there is evidence to show that greatest benefits are
likely to come from building such new roads as urban motorways'.[4]

The Roads Campaign Council in its pamphleteering pushed the
point home. Predicting 12 million vehicles on the roads by 1963 it
claimed: 'work must begin now to prepare for this flood of vehicles.
Otherwise the wheels of transport, by sheer weight of numbers, will
be slowed to walking pace'.[5]

But despite the enthusiastic support of the ministry's engineers the
road lobby's push was ahead of its time. In 1958, the ministry did
ask councils to prepare plans for urban roads, but the circular had
little effect.[6]

The breakthrough came with the appointment of Ernest Marples
as Minister of Transport in 1959. The SMMT was already in three-
way talks with the ministry and the Treasury over the problems posed
by the increasing number of cars. This group proposed a special study
of urban roads.[7]

Marples, a minister who was perfectly in tune with the ministry's
engineers, took up the idea enthusiastically. He told the Conservative
Party conference in Blackpool in 1960: 'We have to rebuild our cities.
We have to come to terms with the car.'[8] And he praised the BRF
for focusing attention on the problem.[9]

The man Marples selected to head this study was Colin Buchanan, reportedly after he had read Buchanan's book *Mixed Blessing* on a trans-Atlantic flight.[10] Buchanan had been much impressed by German roads: 'I have yet to see anything that has taken my breath away as it was taken away when I first saw the German autobahnen in 1937.'[11] He outlined his approach to the task at a symposium organised by the Roads Campaign Council: 'When I observe a snarl-up of traffic I instinctively ask what can be done by way of physical rearrangement.'[12]

Buchanan's report was published in 1963.[13] The main theme of the report was segregating motor traffic and pedestrians. Even now, apologists point to the more enlightened passages, such as the concept of environmental areas where traffic would be banned, or the finding that it was physically impossible to build enough roads to cater for all the traffic. But in practice it was a charter for urban road building, on an impossibly expensive scale. Even small towns, such as Newbury, an example quoted in the report, were to have their urban motorways, and distributor roads all channelling traffic into the old-fashioned main street.[14]

Certainly Marples had no difficulty in interpreting the report. He told a BRF conference, held to celebrate the publication:

> I am sure the British Road Federation will agree with me. It is fundamental to the whole report that it accepts the motor vehicle as a brilliant and beneficial invention. It is in no sense restricting the motor car. All it says is that we must use our motor cars to the maximum and yet be sensible and keep some good environmental areas. We have to face the fact, whether we like it or not, that the way we have built our towns is entirely the wrong way for motor traffic. We want an entirely different type of town.[15]

At the end of the conference Buchanan told the BRF's chairman: 'What we have to do is to keep up a full head of steam and see that the pressure which has been generated is kept up until we get results.'[16]

The road lobby certainly did its best to keep up the pressure. It held a series of regional conferences to illustrate how the Buchanan principles might be applied locally. The road show's first stop was in Newcastle upon Tyne, where one of the leading speakers was the city boss, T. Dan Smith, who had been a member of Buchanan's steering committee.[17]

The show went on to Glasgow, to Liverpool in 1965, where the leading speaker was naturally the Lancashire county surveyor, James Drake, and finally to Leeds, where the main speaker was the West Riding county surveyor, Maynard Lovell.[18]

The ministry sent out a circular to councils, exhorting them to draw up 'land use transportation plans', an American technique which involved forecasting how much traffic there will be, and then planning the roads to accommodate it. It was a technical device designed to encourage large-scale road building, and it was exclusively concerned with roads, with no parallel attempts to plan for public transport being made until well into the 1970s.[19]

Engineers like Drake and Lovell barely needed any encouragement. But for city engineers in smaller local authorities, such as Nottingham, Portsmouth and Southampton, the circular enormously increased their political leverage by taking transport out of politics, and making it a matter for technical judgment. In the next ten years, more than one hundred councils began land use transportation plans.[20]

The political reaction to these plans was one of almost universal approval. A few Labour politicians did express doubts, but they were a small minority. The highways committees were universally enthusiastic, with Labour councils vying with Tories to build the new roads. Lovell's blind bulldozers were let loose in Leeds and by the mid-1970s Glasgow's main achievement was that it had more motorways and fewer cars per head of population than any other British city.

The biggest battle was to come over London. The city's sheer size means that it dominates transport strategy over much of the country, and it has frequently been a pace-setter for developments in other cities.

Public transport is more important in cities than private transport, at least during rush hours. This is largely a matter of using space efficiently. Cities are crowded. There is little space. A bus can carry seventy people, or more. Transfer all these people to cars, with one or two people per car, and the result is a traffic jam.

Most people commute to city centre jobs by bus, or by train, rather than by car. The bigger the city, the more people use public transport. In London more than eight times as many people travelled to work in the centre by bus or train in 1985 than by car.[21]

The road lobby has always regarded this dependence on public transport as bad. 'Trains and tubes won't give what is needed . . . the people walking in all weathers between their railway or tube stations or their bus or tram stops and their jobs cover an annual distance equal to some 270 000 times the circumference of the earth.' Instead the road lobby wants door to door transport, 'a road plan augments freedom for all'.[22]

The first major road plans for London were put forward by Sir Charles Bressey, the ministry's chief engineer, and Sir Edwin

Lutyens.[23] They proposed a series of ring roads. Their plans were reworked in the 1940s by Sir Patrick Abercrombie[24]. Apart from his ring road proposals, his County of London plan is remarkable because it fails to mention buses, even once.[25]

In 1951, Labour scrapped the plan for the innermost of Abercrombie's ring roads. The A ring would have circled London about two miles from Trafalgar Square. The BRF protested 'its construction would largely solve the present congestion in London'.[26] In its place, the incoming Conservative government decided to turn Park Lane, on the western edge of central London, into a dual carriageway. John Boyd-Carpenter, then Minister of Transport, told the cabinet: 'no single road development scheme could make a greater contribution to the relief of growing traffic congestion'.[27]

Five years after the A ring had been officially dropped, the engineers were still drawing it on their plans. In 1956 Baker and Glanville produced a plan for the M1, showing the London end of the motorway terminating at a vast intersection with the A ring, just to the north of Marble Arch.[28]

However, the London County Council was lukewarm about such expensive plans, despite the 75 per cent government grant which such roads automatically attracted. Even 25 per cent of the cost was a lot of money to put on the rates. So, despite the enthusiasm of its own road engineers,[29] the council was more cautious about large-scale road building, saying that it 'must be linked to levels of annual expenditure'.[30]

This was not good enough for the BRF. Off it scurried in February 1960 to see its friend Ernest Marples. The BRF wanted the council to adopt plans for ringways. Marples subsequently called in the council to discuss its road plans, and to express his concern that the plan did not include ringways.[31]

The council persisted. Its revised development plan, which was published in April, did not include ringways. The BRF objected: 'on the grounds that its highway proposals were inadequate for the known needs of traffic'.[32] At a four and half hour public hearing, the council eventually conceded the point, accepting 'the concept of a motorway system probably in the form of a ring'.[33]

The ministry and the council commissioned a vast survey of where people went to (by car, of course), and why, to help in the planning of the new roads. The BRF had already demanded such a survey.[34] It called the survey 'a step in the right direction . . . the major improvement which the federation will expect is the provision of urban motorways'.[35]

The survey was published in 1963. The ringway plans were taken

13 *The road lobby fought hard to have the M4 built, and transport minister Ernest Marples' firm helped to build it*

over by the GLC when it was created in 1965, enjoying the support of both the first Labour administration and the following Conservative council. For the rest of the 1960s the ringways had all-party support.

A London MP told the House of Commons: 'the witness from the ministry admitted to the committee that all these plans were in fact the result of a series of pressures . . . the strongest lobby is the British Road Federation'.[36]

Henceforth the ministry took a keen interest in London's road plans. Although the ringways are frequently described as the GLC's plans (as indeed they formally were), in reality they were drawn up jointly by the engineers from the ministry and the council. The GLC and the ministry set up a joint steering group in 1965. A year later a joint team of road engineers was set up, in County Hall, to work on the plans. This was an unusual move, underlined by the ministry's concern to keep its engineers in the manner to which they had become accustomed: 'they will expect a standard of accommodation not appreciably lower than that to which they are entitled at the ministry'.[37]

This committed group of engineers drew up their road schemes (which were to be included in the Greater London Development Plan) in almost complete isolation from both the public and other GLC colleagues. The cost of these roads was phenomenal, £2 billion at 1972 prices, which roughly equates to £10 billion at 1986 prices – about three times the cost of the Channel Tunnel.

The devastation was on a scale so vast that it made even the BRF blanche.[38] The ringways would have meant demolishing 20,000 houses in a city which then had a housing shortage of half a million.

The engineers bounced their plans through the GLC's chief architect, who complained, 'it is regrettable, however, that I was not given longer to consider the points raised by the Ministry of Transport'.[39] Two days later the engineers raised the question: 'To what extent should we involve the planning department?'[40]

Only in 1970 was the brief of the council and ministry joint steering group widened, from just road building, to encompass public transport. It was six months before the public inquiry was due to open, and designed to ensure that road plans were changed as little as possible.

However, public opinion was beginning to be alarmed at the scale and devastation that the ringways would cause. There were a number of factors behind this alarm. One was a growing concern about the environment, a desire to conserve Victorian housing, for example. Another was the widespread distrust of 'the planners', people who professed to know best, redeveloped whole areas and manifestly produced housing which was at least as bad as that it replaced – disrupting and destroying a community in the process. The BRF could write of ringway one, the innermost road that became known as the 'motorway box': 'Much of the route lies in obsolete areas which urgently need rebuilding.'[41] It was not a sentiment shared by the people of Blackheath, Chelsea, Hampstead or Kensington, who like their old houses. A third factor was that for the first time a sizeable number of people from the affluent and articulate middle classes were affected.

The fourth factor, which was vital to the success of the campaign against the ringways was the scale of road building and the number of people affected. Public opinion is slow to rouse. But it is rather like a chain reaction. When enough people become concerned, and excited, then like a piece of fissile material, the situation reaches a critical mass. The reaction is then explosive. For four years, from 1969 to 1973, more people began to be concerned about the ringways. The concern mounted until it went off with a bang, wrecking the ringway plans.

The first sign of opposition to road building surfaced in the 1960s. The Chiswick Motorway Liaison Committee was set up to fight the extension of the M4 into London. It failed. In 1969, the government

ran into trouble with its plan for widening Falloden Way, a section
of the A1 in north London. The GLC's road engineers watched the
public inquiry anxiously. They were horrified that it lasted fourteen
days. They were worried about outsiders coming in to oppose the
scheme. (They included people from the Archway Road, who were
worried about the domino effect of road widening on their section of
the A1, and people from Chiswick passing on their experience of
fighting roads.) The engineers at the GLC, however, put down the
opposition to 'a well financed organisation [which] spared no
effort . . . to arouse local feeling'.[42]

A much-better financed organisation, the road lobby, was busy
swaying parliamentary opinion behind the ringways. The Roads
Campaign Council organised at least two meetings in 1968 and 1969
so that the GLC (and doubtless the BRF) could put its plan to MPs.[43]
Douglas Jay, who was then a Labour backbencher, recalls one
occasion:

> They once organised a lunch at County Hall, attended by MPs
> and GLC officials. To MPs it appeared that the GLC were the
> hosts, but when you looked into it you found the hosts were in
> fact the BRF, who produced a fleet of buses to take people across
> Westminster Bridge.[44]

The close operation between the GLC, the government and the
road lobby continued. By 1969 the government and the GLC were
holding monthly progress meetings.[45] The BRF employed Tom
Williams as its consultant.[46] In June 1969, Williams and the GLC
met to discuss twenty-six detailed points about the ringways.
Williams asked for information that would certainly have been
denied to the opposition: 'All I ask is that I have some oral replies
to these questions during our meeting . . . that procedure would . . .
ensure that any classified information should have the minimum of
circulation.'[47]

The smooth run-up to the public inquiry was badly jolted by the
publication of *Motorways in London*, a well-researched attack on the
whole principle of the ringways, produced by a working party led by
Michael Thomson, a transport economist.[48] It was exactly the sort of
study which the road lobby and the government had a monopoly on,
up until then. Alarm bells rang at the road lobby.

Phillipson, the BRF's director, was quickly on the phone to John
Fitzpatrick, the GLC's assistant director of planning and transportation, to ask for help. Within 24 hours Fitzpatrick wrote back, in a
letter headed 'confidential':

'Dear Phillipson,
As arranged on the telephone I enclose some comments on
Motorways in London. They are only first thoughts and initial
technical reactions. You appreciate they are not intended for
publication and they do not represent the council's considered
view on this book. However, I hope that the comments on this
book will serve your immediate purpose.[49]

There followed ten pages of detailed criticism of Thomson's book.[50]

In an attempt to dampen down the opposition, the GLC hired
Colin Buchanan's consultancy firm to put an environmental gloss on
its plans.[51] In the same year the BRF also commissioned Buchanan's
firm to study the future road plans of Britain's biggest cities.[52]

Buchanan himself was firmly in favour of ringways. 'I refuse to
believe that London which is man-made and has been remade several
times in the course of its existence, could not be remade again to
accommodate the motorways in a successful manner.'[53]

But the ringways were fast ceasing to be a technical problem. They
were becoming a major political issue. Even before the public inquiry
opened, candidates supporting a platform of Homes before Roads
stood at the 1970 GLC election. They received a total of 71,000
votes, or 1.5 per cent of the poll as the BRF sneered.[54]

This was scarcely a measure of the strength of anti-ringway feeling
in London. The GLC had expected 2,500 objections to the Greater
London Development Plan. It received 22,000. The vast majority of
these objections were opposed to the road plans.

The inquiry, which was chaired by Frank Layfield, who later
chaired the Sizewell nuclear power station inquiry, went on for more
than a year. It was the first major long public inquiry, and became a
trial of strength between the GLC and the opposition, headed by
the London Amenity and Transport Association and the London
Motorway Action Group.[55]

The opening of the Westway, an elevated motorway which ploughs
through north Kensington, brought these protests into focus. The
formal opening, by Michael Heseltine, was disrupted. Banners
proclaimed the motorway 'a monstrous crime'.[56]

The disruption galvanised officialdom into action. The GLC calculated that better compensation would buy off the protesters. A top-
level meeting between the minister and Robert Vigars, who chaired
the GLC's transport committee, was swiftly arranged. Vigars bluntly
told the minister that the GLC would not build the ringways unless
compensation was improved.[57] The government promised action, and
legislation improving compensation was passed in 1973.

Inside County Hall, the GLC was acquiring a bunker mentality. Even friends were hostile. John Nott, a Tory MP at the time, nearly complained in public about a misleading article written by Desmond Plummer, the GLC leader, in defence of the motorway box. Nott held back at the last minute: 'nothing looks worse than Tories having a disagreement in public'.[58]

The GLC began to clutch at straws. The Kensington Society was one of the few local groups to support the ringways. Vigars wrote: that it was 'one of the oldest *genuine* amenity societies as distinct from those that have sprung up with the object of opposing the ringways'.[59]

The decisive political fight over the ringways was now taking place in the Labour Party. Many of the old guard still supported the ringways.[60] But in 1971, the London Labour Party came out against the ringways, much to the Tories' fury: 'they have always supported some form of ringway scheme'.[61]

In the 1973 GLC elections, Labour campaigned on a 'stop the motorways' platform. The Liberals also opposed the ringways. The Conservatives were alone in supporting the plan.

The BRF did its best to help. It launched a £12,000 newspaper campaign, urging voters to support the ringways. The adverts posed the rhetorical question, 'who will benefit the most from London's roads?'. The answer was Londoners – and not the road lobby.

Although this was a vast sum of money to spend on advertising by environmentalists' standards – only £15,000 had been spent on the entire campaign against the ringways – it had little effect on votes. Labour won the elections decisively. Many of the wards straddling controversial sections of the route produced higher than average swings to Labour.

The Layfield inquiry had in the meantime recommended that ringway one, the most damaging of the roads, should be kept and the rest dropped. But this was now irrelevant. The Labour GLC dropped the ringways under its control. The outermost ringway, ringway three, was unaffected by this decision because it lay outside the GLC's jurisdiction.

The scrapping of the ringways was the road lobby's biggest defeat. And it was a defeat that went wider than just the loss of some lucrative road building in London. Roads had ceased to be a technical issue, and instead became involved with party politics.

For the next three or four years the road lobby had no credible political strategy in London. It set up a working party on roads in London, chaired by Sir Alex Samuels, the traffic adviser to the ministry during the late 1960s. The AA was conerned that Samuels' appointment might make the working party too closely identified with the RAC's line.[62]

But, apart from calling for more road spending in London, the road lobby could do little else. The Conservatives were prepared to support higher road spending. But no political party was now willing to espouse the cause of the ringways. And the election of a Labour government removed the possibility that the ministry might assist the road lobby in calls for a return to the ringways.

The road lobby did not return to the attack, and then somewhat warily, until the run up to the 1977 GLC election. The BRF's London group, now called Movement for London, circulated candidates with details of its plans for new roads, and reported an encouraging response.[63]

Andrew Warren, Movement for London's secretary, went on the usual round of Rotary Clubs. The group produced 150,000 copies of a leaflet saying 'The GLC doesn't like motorists', which were distributed to motorists through garages.[64]

The return of the Tories to County Hall in 1977 did not produce any dramatic change in policy, although engineers did begin to work up a new scheme for the West Cross Route, the western side of the motorway box, under the new name of the West London Relief Road. But even this was deferred, because of government spending cuts.[65]

However, in 1980 the road lobby struck back. A group of road engineers from the GLC and the home counties, operating under the banner of the Standing Conference on London and the South East Regional Planning, drew up a £2.5 billion spending programme (1979 prices) for London's roads.[66]

By 1981, Labour was back in power at County Hall. The Labour Party's transport policy had been heavily influenced by environmental groups, such as the London Amenity and Transport Association. It adopted a policy of no increase in the carrying capacity of London's roads, much to the annoyance of many of the council's own road engineers. This marked a considerable success for the environment lobby, and a major setback for the road lobby.

The road lobby mobilised its forces behind the £2.5 billion programme. In the first instance it took its campaign to the House of Commons' transport committee. The interests of this committee were finely balanced. On the Labour side were two MPs sponsored by the National Union of Railwaymen, who were scarcely friends of the road lobby. One of the leading lights on the Conservative side was Peter Fry, the MP for Wellingborough who is joint chairman of the All Party Roads Study Group, and a member of the RAC's public affairs committee.[67] The committee decided to investigate transport in London, following an early study when it called London's roads 'a national scandal'.[68]

The committee's report was published in 1982. It called for a ten-year road action programme, to carry out the Standing Conference's plan. It also called for a public transport action programme and the transfer of buses, tubes and roads to a new metropolitan transport authority.

The motive for this last proposal was to remove road building from party politics. As Fry explained, when arguing against a government takeover of London's roads: 'We all know it takes a lot longer than four or five years to get a new road off the ground, and under the present proposals we might end up with just as disastrous a situation as we have had for the last twenty years.'[69]

The public transport action programme was consigned to instant oblivion. The Department of Transport decided to take over London's roads itself, rather than setting up a new body, arguing: 'the record of the GLC is particularly unsatisfactory. They have done little to improve the quality of the roads for which they are responsible'.[70] The BRF's new London man, Jeremy Hawksley, was ecstatic: 'This is good news for all London motorists'.[71]

In the 1983 general election, the Tories promised to abolish the GLC, a scheme which meshed neatly with their desire to take over London's roads. After a reshuffle, occasioned by the resignation of Cecil Parkinson, Nicholas Ridley became Secretary of State for Transport.

Ridley was a gift for the road lobby, the most sympathetic minister since Marples. Like Marples he had a civil engineering background, and curiously, given his enthusiasm for building roads in London, he was the grandson of Sir Edwin Lutyens. On the libertarian wing of the Conservative Party, Ridley hated wheel clamps, one-way streets (because they interfered with the democratic rights of motorists)[72] and once said he wanted to get rid of half London's traffic lights – presumably the red lights.[73] His ministry was marked by his desire to cut public spending and his even greater enthusiasm for increasing road spending. He achieved both aims by cutting public transport back.

The initial plan was for the Department of Transport to take over 70 miles of the most important roads from the GLC, with the rest going to local councils.[74] The 70-mile network was chosen because the Standing Conference had selected these roads for widening. In the final version, the department gained effective control of a further 300 miles of road, having a veto on anything which impeded the flow of traffic, from bus lanes to zebra crossings.[75]

14 *'The private motorist . . . wants the chance to live a life that gives him a new dimension of freedom – freedom to go where he wants, when he wants, and for as long as he wants'* – Nicholas Ridley

By now the Department of Transport's plans were beginning to cause unrest in the areas which might be affected by road widening. The GLC and environmental groups warned of the extent of the government's plans. The department, wary of stirring up controversy, tried to dampen the disquiet with a mixture of evasion and half truths.

Lynda Chalker, the junior minister who was the acceptable face of the Department of Transport, wrote to residents in Chelsea denying that the government takeover meant that roads were to be widened.[76] 'The suggestion that government's proposals mean a vast programme of motorway building in London is the product of some very fertile imagination.'[77] She said later that tales of 'vast motorway building schemes and increased traffic' were 'mischievous propaganda'.[78] The BRF repeated its call for more road building.[79] At the top of its shopping list were the South Circular Road, the West London Relief Road and a link between east London and the A1 to replace the northern arm of the motorway box.

In the autumn of 1984, Ridley announced four 'assessment' studies: three affected roads on the BRF's list; the fourth was the extension of the M23 into London.

The department was very cagey about what these studies were about. They were certainly designed to discover what local problems were. But the government stuck religiously to its line. It was not going to build ringways. And it tried to imply that this meant no major road building.

Chalker said that 'scaremongering stories' were creating

> unnecessary alarm among ordinary people by claiming that government have plans for major new road schemes in London. That is simply not true. I wish to deal with once and for all the allegations that we are intending to revive the old major road schemes. There will be no motorway box, no ringway roads.[80]

The terms of reference that the department gave its consultants were, however, quite clear. They laid down the aim of 'dealing more effectively with the flow of essential traffic'. At the same time they had to take account of the government public transport policy, which was to cut subsidies, and drive people off the buses and into private cars.

Ridley also reconvened a technical committee and asked it to look at ways of justifying new road building in London. He reappointed Tom Williams, the engineer who had worked for the BRF fifteen years before and who was a member of the RAC's public policy committee, to chair this committee.

Typically, Ridley was less guarded about his intentions. 'It will not mean a motorway programme. Flyovers, underpasses, widening schemes and some new stretches of road are more likely.'[81]

In 1985, to the acute embarrassment of the Department of Transport, the auditor general revealed that road spending in London was due to rise by 1.5 billion, to a total of £2.5 billion. In a letter to a Tory backbencher, Lynda Chalker tried to explain this away:

> I quite understand your concern at the apparent incompatibility of the statement in the comptroller and auditor general's report with my repeated assurance that trunking will not result in large-scale road improvements. Whatever the outcome of the assessment studies there will be no motorway building. . . . That said, you will naturally expect me to go on to say the facts and figures in the report . . . must be wrong. However, I cannot fault the accuracy of the report.[82]

Chalker's explanation was that the figure represented what the department would need to spend if it carried out the transport committee's recommendations.

15 A traffic jam – the motor industry's most potent symbol of success

6 Motorway mania

The doors burst open at the back of the tiny town hall. Two chairs which had been jamming the door handles splintered and fell away. In rushed an angry crowd, led by a local farmer. It was the ninth day of the public inquiry into the Aire Valley motorway.[1]

Breaking down the doors in that Yorkshire town hall of Shipley did not just bring the Aire Valley inquiry to a timely halt. It marked a profound change in public attitudes. The men (and they almost all were) from the ministry had striven desperately to keep the public in its place: to ensure that issues were too technical to be easily understood; to hide behind expert opinion; to patronise anyone who tried to peek through the mystifying veil.

Suddenly, through the doors of Shipley town hall flooded a tide of people who had gained the self-confidence to challenge the unchallengeable. No longer were they to be fobbed off by technicalities, or defeated by rules that loaded the dice in the ministry's favour.

From the Aire Valley to Winchester a succession of inquiries was disrupted. John Tyme, an environmental lecturer at Sheffield Polytechnic, emerged as the leader of this movement, terrorising the ministry and the road lobby. Wherever he went, disruption was sure to follow.

Underlying this groundswell of public opinion were a number of different factors. One was the growth of environmentalism, which is usually dated from the publication, in the United States, of Rachel Carson's book, *The Silent Spring*.

One symptom of this mood was a new wave of environmental groups, such as the Conservation Society, which was set up in 1966, and the more radical Friends of the Earth, which was set up in 1970. Transport 2000, exclusively concerned with transport, was set up in 1972 by an alliance of the railway unions and environmental groups.

More specifically, the struggle over London's ringways had demonstrated that it was possible to take on the road builders – and win. The lesson was quickly learnt in communities throughout the country.

Another spin-off from the ringway struggle was a number of people who had become politicised and acquired experience of fighting road schemes. This fund of expertise became centred on the national environmental groups. Groups such as Friends of the Earth and the Council for the Protection of Rural England, which had been set up as long ago as 1926, were forced (sometimes reluctantly) to take an interest in road building simply because of the number of calls for help they received from members of the public.

Finally the road building programme became a victim of its scale. By the early 1970s road schemes were affecting enough people across the country for public opinion to be roused in exactly the same way that it had been in London. Again, part of the reason was that motorways were now threatening many middle-class communities, if anything more so outside London where many of the worst-affected areas were poor. The middle classes were well equipped to defend themselves. At inquiry after inquiry, local communities would produce their own traffic experts, their own legal experts as well as the often more effective barrack room lawyers, who would run rings round the mandarins from Marsham Street.

It was the first time, certainly since the war, that the road lobby had an opposition to face, and it was baffled. The FTA, with its characteristic gift for understatement said the country was on the verge of 'an amenity civil war'.[2] Faced with this tide of opposition, the road lobby was slow to respond. The lobby's forte was lobbying politicians and civil servants, a word in the ear, a road built here. Its resources and staff were concentrated in London. And its attempts at public campaigning, despite the roads crusade of the 1950s, looked pathetically thin when faced with any substantial opposition.

In 1973, the BRF decided to set up a network of local groups:

> This change in emphasis of the BRF programme has been deliberate. . . . By putting forward a reasoned and well-argued case the groups are helping to counterbalance the views of those instinctively opposing local road schemes, and have already won the support of many local MPs, councillors and the public.[3]

There were initially four local groups, centred on the biggest cities. But this expanded to nine or more in the late 1970s.[4] Each group was formed by rounding up the local BRF members, such as the AA and the RAC, with perhaps an industrial group, such as the chamber of commerce, thrown in. Each group also had its figurehead: in the case of SWORD, the South Western Organisation for Road Development, it was Maynard Lovell, who had moved from Yorkshire to Somerset to retire.

From the beginning the BRF tried to project these groups as independent, referring to them as including 'BRF members' and having 'established close working relationships with the BRF' but that 'each group is independent of the BRF'.[5] However, the local secretary of these groups was, in each case, a full-time staff member, and sometimes the groups had a hazy existence. The secretary of SWORD, for instance, declined to produce the group's minute book at the public inquiry into the North Devon Link Road, recording when the group took the decision to support the road. When he was pressed about who paid his wages the reply was almost a whisper: 'The British Road Federation.'[6] At an inquiry in the Midlands, the secretary of the Midlands Road Development Group, Christopher Milner, would only concede to the BRF having an 'avuncular interest'.[7]

The main aim of this tactic seems to have been to present the groups as an authentic slice of local opinion, which happened to support roads. In Manchester, the BRF chose a name (the Surface Transport Action Group) seemingly designed to create confusion in the minds of casual observers, who would be used to seeing the well-established Greater Manchester Transport Action Group object to new roads. However, in the Midlands this tactic backfired. The M40 Road Group was forced to change its name to the M40 Support Group after it was inundated with calls for help fighting the road.

However, the BRF's director, Robert Phillipson, denied that the links between the local groups and the parent organisation were secret. 'Every group has been launched at a local press conference at which the BRF's interest has been openly stated.'[8] This is just as well, because SWORD's inaugural press release does not mention the BRF.[9]

In the face of growing public pressure, the road lobby became increasingly hysterical. One objector in North Devon, who had written to the local papers making the point that SWORD was a vested interest, received an extremely bombastic letter from the group:

I have to ask you to furnish me with the following information:

1 Have you placed before the Chief Constable of Devon and Cornwall any evidence, factual or otherwise, to support your allegation of any so-called vested interest by SWORD in the North Devon link road? and:

2 Will you appear at the public enquiry into the first stage of the link road and allow yourself to be cross-examined closely on the statements you have made against the link road? You will appreciate, no doubt, that if I do not hear from you by December 31, one conclusion only can be drawn from your published remarks.[10]

Fortunately the chief constable was never troubled with SWORD's squabble.

The BRF's problem was that its local groups enjoyed no significant local support. The environmentalists, on the other hand, were almost all local and vastly outnumbered the local road lobby officials. These officials, however, had some sway with local councillors and were able to generate favourable news coverage, out of all proportion to their local support. The transparent attempts to project these groups as independent also ended up harming their image, as baiting the road lobby became the one cruel sport that everyone in the environment lobby could indulge in with a clear conscience.

Inside the road lobby the staff became extremely frustrated. This frustration found its outlet in a series of letters to the press from road lobby staff, from private addresses, and without mentioning their connection with the BRF. In one case the BRF's London man wrote an official article, replying to a previous anti-M25 piece. The week after this article a letter from a private address in Kent was published enthusiastically endorsing the BRF's point of view. It was written by the secretary of SWORD.[11]

Inevitably the tactic backfired, and the gossip columns had a field day. After another incident, the *Guardian*'s diary rang the BRF employee at work to ask him if it was policy to write such letters: 'I would rather not comment on that', replied the wretched man.[12]

However, the road lobby's local groups were not without their successes. Undermining John Tyme was one of their chief concerns. Their greatest success came at the inquiry into the Ipswich bypass, part of the A45 linking the Midlands with the port of Felixstowe.

Throughout 1976 and 1977, Christopher Milner, the BRF's man in the Midlands, organised support for the road. The Transport and General Workers' Union promised its support, as did the Ipswich Industrial Group and the Haven Club, whose members included MPs and senior management from ports on the east coast.[13]

Tyme visited Ipswich in 1977. Local industrialists published a declaration supporting the road (and asking for an inquiry without disturbances). The Ipswich Industrial Group distributed 20,000 'we want a southern bypass' car stickers, paid for out of a £100 a head whip round.[14].

Public inquiries in the 1970s had a fixed pattern. John Tyme would stand up at the beginning and make a lengthy procedural objection to the inquiry opening at all. The inspector would thank him and then try to get on with the inquiry, telling Tyme that his remedy was in the court. Tyme would say he could not afford the courts and surely the inspector was not going on with an inquiry that might be illegal. The inspector would insist, and disruption followed.

But, at the Ipswich inquiry, the crowd was swollen not so much by objectors to the road but by executives from local firms who had been given the day off to attend the inquiry. Drum majorettes paraded through the town in support of the road.[15]

Emboldened by this show of support, the inspector, Frank Clinch, a retired local authority road engineer, adopted a tough line. He told Tyme to shut up, and threatened to have him thrown out. Tyme chained himself to a large stout table and continued to try to make his objection. The police removed Tyme, the chain and the table, to applause from the executives in the audience.

But Ipswich was an exception. The road lobby was faced with forces which were beyond its control, which could not be manipulated and which it could not understand.

The road lobby's lack of understanding of what it was up against shone through in its criticism. It veered from decrying the opposition for being a minority to being a front for a vested interest, both charges which fitted the road lobby far more accurately. In 1973, the BRF attacked the opposition for being 'really a minority leisure interest with supposedly intellectual overtones'.[16] While its charge of 'elitism' against 'critics of roads and the vehicle' at least had the political purpose of trying to undermine the environmentalists' growing support in the Labour Party.[17] But the lobby was happiest when it could ascribe to the opposition some sinister vested interest. In the road lobby's demonology, the rail unions ranked as the satan in chief. So the opposition to the M25 stemmed from 'professional objectors' and the 'scaremongering of the tiny minority railway lobby'.[18]

The rise of environmentalism and public opposition to roads also worried the ministry. At first ministers pushed ahead with business as usual. Peter Walker, the Secretary of State for the Environment, who in 1972 was the overlord of the transport ministry, told the *Birmingham Post*:

> Roads are our economic lifelines. . . . If our industry is to prosper, if we are to meet the challenge of the common market, a high speed strategic route network is absolutely necessary.[19]

The Labour Party came to power in 1974. But although the London Labour Party was set against major road building, this more sceptical approach was not shared by the party at Westminster, nor by many local Labour parties outside the capital. Under Tony Crosland, the Secretary of State for the Environment, and John Gilbert, the minister who was directly in charge of transport, Labour's road policy was indistinguishable from that of the Tories.

The oil crisis of 1973–4, when petrol doubled in price over a matter of months, gave the road builders a severe jolt, and gave more weight to the environmentalists' arguments. But this produced no immediate change in policy. Crosland concurred with the BRF in thinking that environmentalists were middle-class people who wanted 'to pull up the ladder behind them'.[20] Gilbert was a keen motorist and refused even to see groups which wanted to argue against the road programme.

The appointment of Bill Rodgers as Secretary of State for Transport did bring a change. His junior minister, who took charge of the roads programme, was John Horam, who before becoming a minister had appeared at a public inquiry to argue against a road going through Newcastle upon Tyne.

Rodgers set about removing the 'genuine grievances' of those who opposed roads. [21] He set up an inquiry into public inquiries, to draw up rules that would be fairer. He also set up another inquiry to study the technical justification for roads (such as traffic forecasts) which had been a source of complaint among objectors.

Labour also began to cut back the road programme significantly. The cuts were forced on it by a more general need to cut public expenditure. But it was the first time since the 1950s that the road programme had to bear its share of the cuts.

There were two cuts in the road programme in 1975, followed by a further three in 1976, culminating in an announcement by Chancellor Denis Healey, under pressure from the International Monetary Fund, of a six-month moratorium on letting motorway building contracts.

The department's road engineers managed to slip through £20 million of road contracts the day before Healey made his speech, and a further £11 million that was not announced until five days afterwards. When confronted with this ploy the department said: 'Fair enough. We need to keep the programme ticking over, and a stop and start system is bad for everyone.'[22]

A more significant defeat for the road lobby came with the publication of the white paper on transport policy in 1977. Tony Crosland had initiated a review of transport policy on taking office because he found that the government had none. A green paper was published in 1976, followed by a period of consultation. But when Rodgers took office practically no work on the policy had been done.

A special team in the department was set up to coordinate work on the policy. The transport policy review unit contained several of the brighter civil servants in the department, and was noticeably free of road engineers.[23]

The period of consultation became a set piece battle between the rival road and environment philosophies. The environment groups wanted a better deal for public transport. The BRF argued predictably that 'the strategic road programme should be the top transport priority and should continue as fast as funds allow with a target date of 1985'.[24]

The battle outside the department was mirrored by another parallel fight inside the department. John Horam recalls that there was resistance from the road engineers to any review of policy: 'The attitude was "we have a policy. The plans are laid. We just have to push them through".'[25]

John Jukes, the director general of highways, wanted the government to continue to support the strategic network, which then stood at 4,500 miles. The green paper was remarkably emphatic, given its status as a consultation paper. 'In England about 2,000 miles of the strategic network of motorways and trunk roads has now been completed. A further 1,000 miles is regarded as of high priority.'[26]

The road engineers' strategy was to avoid any discussion of roads policy. The ministers and all the senior civil servants at the department spent a weekend at Sunningdale to discuss the content of the white paper. Although the roads programme was by far and away the largest slice of the department's spending, the policy was not discussed at all. Indeed originally Jukes had not even wanted a chapter on roads in the white paper, according to one report.[27]

When the draft of the chapter on roads arrived, Horam took it home and changed it. The engineers were outraged. The white paper opted for a more 'flexible approach', instead of a rigid adherence to a strategic network, and cut a further £60 million off the roads budget.[28] Jukes retired.

The government produced two other sops for the environmentalists. The review of public inquiries recommended giving objectors more information.[29] The inquiry into the technical justification of road schemes criticised the department's methods of forecasting.[30]

The 1978 white paper on roads dropped thirty-four road schemes, an unheard of departure from previous practice. Roads had been deferred before, but rarely dropped. The M67, for example, planned to link Manchester and Sheffield, just fell off the road engineers' map.[31]

The road between Birmingham and Oxford, which would have been an 'automatic choice' for a motorway was downgraded, but only after a lengthy fight between the ministers and the engineers.

Even then the engineers did not finally concede defeat. The M40 extension became the X40 – with the X standing for a standard that had yet to be chosen.

The government's decision in the late 1970s to route the M1 east of Leeds infuriated the road lobby. The choice was between a route that bisected Leeds and Bradford, the 'blue route', and one to the east of Leeds. In the public consultation exercise, 70 per cent of local residents favoured the route east of Leeds.

Horam went up to inspect the route, in a coach, accompanied by representatives of various local groups as well as reporters. The blue route went straight through Wharfedale, a local beauty spot. He was horrified and decided immediately that the M1 would have to go east of Leeds.

At one of the regular meetings that ministers hold with their engineers and county surveyors, at Harrogate, Horam announced his decision that the road would go east of Leeds. The engineers were outraged. The county surveyor of North Yorkshire, Colonel Gerry Leech, stood up and said: 'But minister you can't do that.' He argued that the road had been planned to run through Wharfedale for ten years, and it was far too late to change the route now.

Although Horam was persuaded to retreat to having made a 'provisional' decision, the road lobby was horrified, blaming it on the result of public consultation. Phillipson, the BRF's director, objected to the delay that a new route would cause:

> Public participation is providing a ready weapon for delay – and downright disruption – in the hands of determined minorities. . . . This shows, in probably the worst single decision of its type, the pure lunacy of public participation.[32]

The BRF's answer was to set up a new local group, the Blue Route Action Group (BRAG), to push for the original route. A letter, signed by the BRF's local woman (although failing to mention this connection, and written from the address of the Bradford Chamber of Commerce), was sent to likely supporters. The link between this group and the BRF was revealed by a local anti-road group. When taxed with it, on local radio, the BRF woman replied: 'there is no conflict of interest between my working for BRAG and the BRF. We are all interested in building roads'.[33] Naturally.

By 1979, road spending had fallen to nearly half, in real terms, of what it had been when Labour took office. And Horam was talking of the end of the motorway programme being in sight. While the road lobby was in retreat, the environment lobby, from being ostracised by the department, was now welcomed at every level from ministers downwards.

However, Labour had to come to terms with the road construction interests, who argued to ministers that they needed a steady programme, and wanted to avoid cycles of boom and bust. The biggest symbol of this steady programme was the M25 around London. It went ahead as though road building had never gone out of fashion, largely because ministers decided that too much of it had been built to stop it.

For the road lobby, the steady programme was a spring board to greater road spending. The BRF said it was 'no time to stop',[34] as the general election approached. Its proposals were based on those presented in 1979 by the County Surveyors' Society, to MPs at a meeting of the All Party Roads Study Group. The surveyors said 'the absolute decline in road building . . . should be reversed'.[35]

The Conservatives were returned to power in the general election of 1979. Norman Fowler, the new Secretary of State, was more sympathetic to the road lobby, even to the extent of expounding his new Tory transport policy at a BRF fringe meeting at the Tory Party conference in 1977.[36]

However, government policy was slow to change. Rodgers and Horam continued to have an influence on policy long after they ceased to be ministers. The road engineers were somewhat bruised by their clash, and wary.

As late as 1982, the county surveyors' pleas for higher road spending were rejected by the department, on the grounds that the surveyors were just pushing their pet schemes.[37] And Kenneth Clarke, Fowler's junior minister, repeated the vision of an end to motorways, although the end had receded noticeably:

> Obviously we are not far away from the end of the motorway
> building programme . . . there will come a stage and it is
> probably a decade or so away, where those routes that justify
> links of motorway standards will be more or less complete.[38]

And he forecast that the road between Birmingham and Oxford, now upgraded once again to a motorway, would be the last one.

It was not a verdict which the road lobby was ever likely to accept. The House of Commons transport committee (on which Peter Fry is an influential member) said that motorways were needed 'on a rather larger scale' than the government thought, and recommended an increase in road spending.[39]

Under a Conservative government, the BRF began to recover its composure. The drop in road building had reduced the number of major inquiries. John Tyme had gone to live in Gloucestershire, in semi-retirement. And the disruption of yet another inquiry ceased to be newsworthy. Public opinion was no longer concerned about roads. By 1983, the BRF felt confident enough to start publishing its annual report again, which it had stopped in 1977, when the political tide was running strongly against it.

The BRF had also been forced to cut back on its activities because of its own cash crisis. The cuts largely fell on the local groups, which had never been one of the BRF's more successful enterprises.

Ten years previously, the road lobby had successfully raised the road building target and, in a pincer movement, accelerated the rate of road building. Now it tried to repeat the old one two.

The civil engineering group of the National Economic Development Organisation began studying how to cut down the time taken to build a road. The first report from this group recommended a considerable reduction in the right to object at public inquiries, although this was toned down in the group's final report. But the government backed away from action, for fear of provoking an environmental backlash.[40]

However, the road lobby had more success with its bid for higher road spending. It was helped by the appointment of Nicholas Ridley as Secretary of State for Transport in 1983.

In 1984, the BRF and the Federation of Civil Engineering Contractors organised a conference to peddle their demands for higher spending on roads. The CBI called for an additional £3 billion to be spent on roads, over ten years, while the BRF's London man, Jeremy Hawksley, wanted £3 billion spent in London alone.

George Henderson, the national construction secretary of the Transport and General Workers' Union, said that both the CBI and the BRF were being too modest. Len Payne, from the FTA, said that 'all the concerned organisations need now to come together and get the message across'.[41]

By 1985, Ridley was able to tell the CBI that it now had what it wanted, although the transport workers could scarcely expect any joy from him. He said that road spending had increased by nearly 30 per cent in real terms since 1979 and that he had met 'almost all the CBI's demands to improve the road network'.

Ridley said that, in June 1985, fifty-one schemes, worth £300 million, had been added to the road programme.

> Of these schemes eighteen (worth £140 million) were located on roads specifically identified in your report as needing improvement. . . . With very few exceptions we now have improvements planned for all of the routes identified by the CBI . . . it strikes me that . . . when we examine the details there is very little that you want that we are not doing.[42]

7 Forty tonnes – what do you bet?

Two days before the end of 1944, the road lobby sent the government its demands for heavier lorries. The lobby wanted longer and wider lorries. It wanted their speed limits increased (from 20 to 30 mph). It wanted the limit on axle weights, then standing at 8 tons, abolished. And it wanted an increase in the maximum weight from 22 to 40 tons.[1]

The Ministry of Transport reacted cautiously to such sweeping proposals. The main stumbling block was the ministry's road engineers. They feared that heavier lorries would break up the roads and that wider lorries would be too big for many streets. It was eleven months before the ministry met the SMMT and the National Road Transport Federation (an alliance of bus and lorry operators) to discuss this shopping list.[2]

The ministry told the lobbyists that increasing lorry speeds 'was viewed sympathetically'. However, the engineers insisted that an axle weight limit stayed. On the ministry's initiative a joint committee was set up, of the ministry, the federation and the SMMT, to study future rules.

Then, as now, the speed limit was widely ignored by lorries. The civil service was complacent, arguing that there was 'no evidence that accidents result from vehicles exceeding the speed limit'.[3]

The ministry consulted its road safety committee in April 1946. 'In view of the fact that the 20 mph limit is largely ignored . . . the committee may consider that to defer the concession . . . will make no practical difference', was the ministry's line.[4]

But the ministry did not tell the committee about other parts of the package, including the idea of increasing weights. The committee agreed to higher speeds with some reluctance, recommending that they be strictly enforced.[5]

Having decided to raise the limits, the ministry was determined to slip them through with as little fuss as possible. The Transport and General Workers' Union had to be told – it was after all a Labour government – but this was delayed for six months, until the start of 1947. Inside the ministry the question was:

> Do you think it is necessary to write to anyone else; the highway authorities are probably the next most interested but if we go to them we must consider other road users (motoring clubs, cyclists, etc) and the whole caboodle. I suggest we elicit the union view and then put it to the society and the NRTF. . . . [6]

It was the union that upset this cosy arrangement. The leadership was initially amenable. But many members were not, having been stirred up by a campaign, according to the ministry. The union objected because 22-ton vehicles 'would constitute a grave public danger if speed was increased'.[7]

The ministry did not sympathise with the union's point of view. It thought drivers broke the speed limit just to get longer breaks.[8] At a meeting between the ministry and the SMMT, the union and the federation, civil servants confronted the union with evidence of speeding. 'Observations . . . on several main roads' showed that few lorries obeyed the limit. The ministry had counted only forty lorries.[9]

By the autumn of 1947, the row had reached the ears of the municipalities, who wondered why they had not been consulted. The ministry took legal advice in an attempt to avoid wider consultations. The minister had to consult 'such representative organisations as he sees fit', ran the advice, 'I suggest that this obligation has been discharged . . .'[10]

But the ministry had been caught out, and it was forced to back down. 'We really have no alternative but to publish the proposals widely.' The ministry (with extreme reluctance) was even forced to include the Pedestrians' Association in its consultation – because it had protested to MPs about the plans.

In June 1948, at a chance meeting over dinner, the Minister of Transport, Alfred Barnes, was much impressed by the managing director of Albion Motors. He argued that the export prospects for his vehicles would be damaged without higher domestic speeds. Barnes secured Cabinet support. And Herbert Morrison, the Lord President, backed a strategy to minimise criticism.[11]

But the union dug its heels in, despite being leant on by ministers. The road lobby kept up the pressure, with a series of deputations from the BRF, the SMMT, and the RHA, as well as the Federation of British Industries and the National Union of Manufacturers (both now part of the CBI). In 1950, nearly 200 MPs signed a motion calling for higher speeds.[12]

The election of a Conservative government in 1951 did not immediately improve the prospects for higher speeds. The Conservatives had close links with the road lobby as the result of the campaign against the nationalisation of road transport. 'No doubt Churchill is committed up to the hilt to the road hauliers', as Richard Crossman put it. [13] But the government was now denationalising road haulage, and it did not want to antagonise the unions further.

In 1953, the government finally promised a BRF deputation that it would force through higher speed limits. The meeting agreed: 'in order not to cause any premature disclosure of what had occurred, an innocuous and unrevealing press release would be made ... the delegation would maintain strict confidence about what the minister had said'.[14]

The death of the union's general secretary, Arthur Deakin, delayed the regulations further. The government waited for Frank Cousins to be elected, to obtain his consent. [15] The change finally came in 1957. The BRF held a celebratory lunch. The guest of honour was the Minister of Transport, Harold Watkinson.[16]

Meanwhile the road lobby continued to press for heavier and larger lorries. At the end of 1947, the ministry consulted on the 'reasonable compromise' which it had agreed with the SMMT and the federation. This time the ministry recognised it would have to consult widely, after its failure to slip through higher speeds on the quiet.[17]

Uncharacteristically, the road lobby fluffed its chance. The SMMT thought it saw a chance of achieving an increase in maximum width as well as weight. Calling the weight increase an 'interim measure of progress', the SMMT said that the weight could not be increased without having a wider lorry.

The approach annoyed the ministry, which felt it had given enough. It decided to tell the SMMT 'flatly', 'we do not intend to increase the maximum width – do you want the weight increase postponed?' [18]

The SMMT stuck to its obviously fallacious argument. The ministry withdrew its proposals. Too late, the National Road Transport Federation tried to retrieve the situation by appealing for an immediate weight increase. But the ministry thought the federation had been put up to it by the SMMT on seeing 'the results of their recalcitrance'.[19]

Lorry weights were not increased until 1955, with the maximum rising from 22 to 24 tons. The width was increased at the same time, by the six inches the SMMT wanted.

This concession simply paved the way for a further set of demands. By 1960 the BRF and the SMMT were calling for an increase in the maximum weight, this time to 28 tons.[20] The opposition to this pressure was far from strong. The Pedestrians' Association tried its best, circulating a scrappy leaflet opposing heavier weights. But it was no match for the road lobby and its increasingly sympathetic allies in the ministry.

In 1964, the ministry raised the maximum weight to 32 tons, and also increased the permitted width and the length. Two years later the ministry gave way to further road lobby pressure and raised the speed limit from 30 to 40 mph. And in 1968 the maximum length of lorries was increased still further, to 15 metres, so that lorries could now carry the largest international containers, which had been standardised at 40 feet (12 metres) long.

Now the road lobby returned to the attack again. It wanted the maximum weight raised, so that these containers could be carried fully loaded. At the time, fully loaded international containers could be carried legally in Britain only on the railways. British Rail was fast developing a network of container services, geared to serve international traffic.

The pattern was the same as every other post-war attempt to relax the restrictions on lorries. First the SMMT went into a huddle with the ministry to discuss the new package. They agreed that the maximum weight for an articulated lorry (the one that most people recognise as a juggernaut) was to be 44 tonnes. The SMMT argued that heavier lorries would cut the cost of transport, and so reduce prices in the shop, as well as boosting exports.

The proposals became public in 1969 – one week after the ministry and the SMMT had denied any knowledge of them.[21] The FTA and the RHA backed heavier lorries. Pedestrians opposed them.

However, this time the weight increase was not a forgone conclusion, once the SMMT and the ministry had set the target. The number of heavy lorries had begun to increase sharply, following the general relaxation of regulations in the 1960s and the end, in 1968, of the strict licensing rules which had kept many heavy lorries off the road.

There was a groundswell of public opinion against heavier lorries, which meshed fortuitously with the increase in environmental awareness. A number of organisations, including the Civic Trust, which had not been closely concerned with transport issues until then, began to voice concern about heavier lorries.

By 1969, the *Sunday Times* had taken up the campaign. It ran a series of articles (under the headline of 'The Juggernauts') arguing against heavier lorries and pointing out the damage they did.[22] It was a theme that other Fleet Street papers took up. Heavy lorries had ceased to be solely a local issue, and become elevated to a national problem.

This movement of public opinion forced a rethink in the ministry.

Richard Marsh, as Minister of Transport, had been prepared 'to give manufacturers the go-ahead on this kind of thing'.[23] But the new minister, Fred Mulley, reacted more cautiously. Under pressure from MPs and local societies, Mully promised to consult widely before raising lorry weights.

Public consultation was exactly what the close links between the road lobby and the ministry had been designed to avoid. Consultation has two effects. The first is to open up an issue to wider public debate. The second, in this case, was that it halted the political momentum to raise lorry weights, if only because the civil servants closely supporting the weight increase had to be diverted to sifting the public's response.

The most effective response was that of the Civic Trust.[24] It carried out a survey of its 750 local societies. Not one supported the increase unconditionally. And the 325 replies provided a horrifying catalogue of the juggernaut's impact.

The incidents ranged from people who had to take sleeping pills to gain any respite from the traffic's roar to one of a lorry squeezing its way through the narrow streets of Chepstow, catching an elderly woman against a wall and crushing her to death.

The Civic Trust's report was a major advance in the sophistication of the arguments against heavier lorries, just as Michael Thomson had provided a similar intellectual argument against the ringways in London.

The Trust pointed out that many of the arguments in favour of heavier lorries were specious. The road lobby had said that heavier weights were needed to 'harmonise' with lorry weights in other European countries. The Trust found that most countries had a maximum weight which was well short of the 44 tonnes demanded by the SMMT.

The consultation produced a wide range of hostile responses, ranging from the Council for the Protection of Rural England through to the Royal Institute of British Architects.

While the consultation process had been going on, the 1970 general election had produced a victory for the Conservatives. Transport came under the Department of the Environment, but the day-to-day dealings were the direct responsibility of John Peyton. Peter Walker, the Secretary of State for the Environment, had close links with the road hauliers, dating from their campaign against Barbara Castle's transport bill three years before. But ministers had to face political realities.

Peyton did a deal with the SMMT. The maximum weight would have to stay at 32 tonnes, for the time being.[25] But in return for easing the pressure for the heaviest lorries, the ministry would change the regulations for other classes of lorry, allowing a general weight increase for all except the largest.[26]

So that while the maximum weight for articulated lorries was unchanged, the weight limit for rigid lorries with four axles went up from 28 to 30 tons, and another 2 tons was added to the maximum weight of lorries with three axles.

The problem for the environmentalists was that public anxiety was fixed on the 32-ton limit because the heaviest lorries worried people most. But the public was less worried about the technicalities of axle loading, or limits for different classes of lorry. Because it was impossible to switch the focus of public concern away from the heaviest lorries, these increases slipped through virtually unopposed.

During this period Britain was negotiating to join the EEC. The original member states of the community had agreed a new weight limit of 40 tonnes. But Peyton successfully argued that Britain should not have 40-tonners forced on it so shortly after joining, although British officials were prepared to agree to higher weights. Peyton's political backbone was stiffened by a resolution passed by the House of Commons that 'this house, mindful of the environment, is against bigger and heavier lorries'.[27]

Despite these setbacks the ministry and the roads lobby had not given up hope of allowing heavier lorries. They were just biding their time. They decided to launch a campaign to promote the image of the heavy lorry.

Peyton said that lorries were the key to 'the good life'.[28] He then asked Sir Dan Pettit, the chairman of the National Freight Corporation, which was then state-owned, 'to assemble an informal group of people concerned with transport to examine the role of road haulage today and its impact on the lives of millions of people who though they may benefit from it greatly resent its intrusions'.[29]

Pettit's group claimed to represent 'a wide cross-section of industry and local government'.[30] Apart from Pettit, who was one of the leading lights in the BRF, and a road engineer from London who was closely involved in designing the ringways, the original team consisted of seven other people. Two were on the board of the RHA; three were on the board of the FTA; another came from a distribution company which had close links with the FTA. The final member was Hugh Featherstone who, like Pettit, was on the BRF's board, and was the chief executive of the FTA.

The conclusion of this independent committee, in a report published at the government's expense, was to take 'the view, as put by the FTA . . . [that] there are few problems that cannot be solved by the provision of roads on the one hand and sensible constraint through traffic management on the other'.[31]

In 1974, the ministry produced a neat sidestep. Two years previously the anti-lorry feeling had helped an MP to push through a private members' bill which allowed councils to ban lorries in certain areas. The ministry turned this idea on its head. Arguing that banning lorries would effectively limit them to a certain number of roads, the ministry came up with the idea of creating lorry routes, which lorries would be encouraged to use.[32]

From the ministry's point of view, lorry routes provided a way of reducing the opposition to heavier lorries (because they could be restricted to designated routes) and at the same time provided an argument for new roads.

The environmentalists came close to buying this plan. Lorry routes, said the ministry, were a way of keeping lorries out of sensitive areas. It was the foresight of one woman, Irene Coates, of the Conservation Society, that put paid to this plan. Coates successfully persuaded the other environmental groups around to her point of view.

The environmentalists' opposition killed off lorry routes and the government finally let the plan lapse. Its only remaining significance is that the plan for lorry routes worked its way into becoming the justification for the county surveyors' network of primary routes.

By the mid–1970s, ministers were still under pressure from the road lobby, the freight directorate and the EEC to allow heavier lorries. Environmentalists were slow to mount an effective presence in Brussels, partly because of the cost of going there, while the road lobby was quick to get its foot in the door.

In 1976, the Department of Transport made another attempt to slip through 40-tonners. It consulted with the road lobby, naturally, but with few other groups. However, the Civic Trust, which had maintained a close interest in road freight and watched developments closely, heard of the plans. Heavier lorries were due to be discussed at an EEC council of transport ministers in March 1977.[33] The Trust alerted local societies, and objections began to pour into the ministry and the EEC. The proposals were shelved.

Two years later, the department tried again. This time Bill Rodgers, who was by now Secretary of State for Transport, discussed heavier lorries with unions and management in road freight. A background note was distributed at the meeting, in which Rodgers said:

> there is a case for implementation of two measures of importance to the efficiency of road transport . . . . Every other EEC country (except Ireland) has a maximum weight of 38 tonnes or more.

Whatever the outcome of EEC attempts at harmonisation – and a successful outcome seems very doubtful would it be inconsistent to raise our maximum weight to 38 tonnes?[34]

Rodgers later denied that he intended to increase the maximum weight and that he 'had any formal consultations of the matter recently'. He said there would be no increase until he was satisfied with 'safety and environmental considerations'.[35]

Three months later, in October 1978, an article appeared in *The Times* arguing for heavier lorries.[36] Rodgers sent the article to Peter Baldwin, the department's top civil servant, with a note suggesting that an inquiry might break the deadlock. Baldwin passed the note to the freight directorate. The head of the freight directorate, Joe Peeler, and his assistant, David Lyness, later discussed the proposal with Baldwin, on Friday 13 October.

As a result of this discussion, Peeler sent a minute to Baldwin's deputy, Peter Lazarus, the following Monday:

> In general we welcome the idea of an inquiry both as a means of getting round the political obstacles to change the lorry weights problem itself, and for wider reasons mentioned in Sir Peter Balwin's [sic] minute. Given that the more straightforward approach is politically unacceptable I have no doubt that the extra time and staff effort needed for the inquiry would be a worthwhile investment.[37]

The minute was duly leaked to Transport 2000, and thence found its way to the *Guardian*.[38] Part of the value of this minute is the light it sheds on attitudes in the civil service, both within the freight directorate, and the attitudes which Peeler expected other civil servants, such as Lazarus (described by the FTA on his retirement as 'an old friend'[39]), to share.

To Peeler, the main purpose of the inquiry was 'presentational':

> At the end of the day recommendations would be made by impartial people of repute who have carefully weighed and sifted the evidence and have come to, one hopes, a sensible conclusion in line with the department's view.
>
> As a subsidiary purpose: It should provide a focus for the various road haulage interests to get together, marshall their forces, and act cohesively to produce a really good case which should not merely establish the main point at issue but should do good to their now sadly tarnished public image. This would make it easier for the government to propose legislation (on lorry weights and other matters) in their favour.

He concluded: 'an inquiry offers a way of dealing with the political opposition to a more rational position of lorry weights'.[40]

Of course there was no guarantee that the inquiry would come to a conclusion 'in line with the department's view', and two further factors were vital. One was the membership of the inquiry, which Peeler did not consider in his minute. The second was the scope of the inquiry. 'A wide-ranging inquiry could be advantageous, and less open to accusations of "rigging", but it would be . . . possibly difficult to keep under control. . . . My own inclination would have been towards a narrowly defined inquiry.'

The *Daily Mirror* in a leading article said that Rodgers 'should tell his officials that their job is to carry out the decisions of Parliament not to try and get round them'.[41] But that is not the way civil servants work, at least in the Department of Transport.

A public opinion poll showed that 79 per cent of people opposed heavier lorries. Only 15 per cent were in favour.[42]

Not that Peeler was one to let up. In an after dinner speech to lorry operators in January 1979 he said: 'the question of lorry weights is very much part of public opinion in this country. I don't wish to enter too much into this controversial issue, but there is a major task of educating public opinion over this issue'.[43] Shortly after this speech Joe Peeler was shifted sharply sideways, to a less controversial job in one of the department's regional offices.

The road lobby kept up its pressure on the government, with the FTA arguing for a maximum weight of 40 tonnes, as a more politically practical target than the 44 tonnes being considered by the SMMT. Rodgers announced that he was going ahead with the inquiry shortly before the 1979 general election, which Labour lost. The new Tory Transport Secretary, Norman Fowler, decided to continue with the inquiry, although he restricted its terms of reference. He appointed Sir Arthur Armitage to head the inquiry.[44]

The inquiry's report was published in December 1980. It was largely drafted by a Department of Transport civil servant, who was subsequently promoted. The report largely accepted the evidence given to it by the road lobby and the Department of Transport (in effect the freight directorate). It backed 44-tonne lorries, although it contained one or two crumbs for the environmentalists, including a plan for 'lorry action areas', to help those worst affected.[45]

The BRF said it was pleased Armitage had supported its arguments. The FTA called the report a £500 million tonic for industry. And they celebrated that evening at a dinner held to celebrate the twenty-fifth anniversary of the Roads Campaign Council. The guest of honour was the Transport Secretary, Norman Fowler, who returned the compliment by announcing a £20 million contract for part of the M25.[46]

However, the government was still wary of public reaction. The FTA urged it to accept the Armitage report, saying that the 44-tonne lorry was 'designed to improve the environment'.[47] The RHA attacked the idea of lorry action areas.[48]

Sir Arthur Armitage also defended his report. He denied that it was designed 'to introduce 44 tonnes'. He denied that his committee was under pressure from the department: 'We were a totally independent inquiry.'[49]

In June 1981, the Labour Party tabled a motion in the House of Commons opposing 44-tonne lorries. The government panicked. It was one of those occasions when it had to take its courage in both hands – and do nothing. It accepted the Labour motion. Fowler was at pains to stress that this did not rule out 40- or even 38-tonne lorries.

Finally, a year after Armitage reported, the government decided to opt for 40-tonne lorries, with the weight spread over five axles, instead of the four axles of the 32-tonner. David Howell, who was by then the new Secretary of State for Transport, promised more bypasses to take lorries out of towns and measures to make lorries 'quieter and cleaner'.[50] He repeated that old road lobby argument that increasing the maximum weight would reduce the number of lorries on the roads. 'You must be joking', commented a Conservative backbencher.[51]

In the debate that followed John Peyton, the former minister, told Howell to 'take the white paper and pulp it'.[52] Eleven backbench Conservatives voted against the weight increase, reducing the government's majority to twenty-nine.

The size of this revolt forced the government to rethink its plans. As Conservative whips tested opinion on the backbenches, ministers and the road lobby began a sustained public relations campaign.

In February 1982, it was the turn of bypasses. Junior minister Kenneth Clarke said that bypasses were 'by far the best way . . . to take lorries away from people'.[53] A week later he repeated the message, while Howell announced eight new bypasses.[54]

The road lobby took up the theme, in a letter to *The Times*, which was signed by the FTA, the RHA, the SMMT and the CBI:

Nowadays we are all environmentalists. . . . We were therefore delighted to see the government's recently announced increased programme of spending on bypasses . . . For the same reason we strongly support government proposals for heavier lorries. . . . [55]

Then the CBI weighed in with an appeal from the director general, Sir Terence Beckett, a former managing director of Ford, directed at waverers on the government's benches:

Along with the Freight Transport Association and the Road Haulage Association, and many individual members, we have talked ourselves hoarse with backbench MPs trying to explain the cost benefits to industry and commerce. . . . We implore MPs on all sides of the house to approve new regulations which we expect to come before the Commons shortly.[56]

In April the accent shifted to improving lorries, linking the improvements to weight increase. New reflective markings would make lorries easier to see. A junior minister said that the new heavier lorries would be safer, on the dubious premise that one manufacturer had just fitted his lorries with anti-skid brakes.[57] The month was rounded off with the ministerial claim that heavier lorries would save 'at least £1.5 billion over the next ten years'.[58]

In May, Howell went to a weighbridge, to see for himself how the existing limits were enforced, and to impress on the public consciousness the government's zeal for enforcing this law.[59] Then he went to see a distribution depot, run by Sainsbury's, a member of the FTA, to see how heavier lorries would help.[60] He finished the month by announcing that he was 'determined to grapple with the heavy lorry issue'.[61] And there the campaign ground to a halt. The announcement of heavier lorries was delayed.[62]

Howell then decided to announce the 38-tonner (as the new limit was going to be) at the Conservative Party Conference at Brighton that autumn. His announcement was distributed to the press before the speech. The SMMT distributed leaflets extolling the virtues of heavier lorries. However, at the last moment, Howell dropped the announcement from his speech. Two pages of his speech were deleted and the official hand-outs were hurriedly retyped.[63]

Even this withdrawal did not save the transport debate from controversy. A former MP who wanted to speak against heavier lorries was prevented from doing so, and walked out protesting that the debate was stagemanaged.

Howell finally gave the go ahead for 38-tonners in November,[64] and the first heavier lorries hit the roads in May 1983. It was the end of the story. And the beginning of another.

For 38 tonnes was never more than a stepping stone to 40- or even 44-tonne lorries for the road lobby. Having pushed hard for a weight increase, the road lobby promptly started complaining that 38-tonne lorries were of little use because the weight of the extra axle (about 1.5 tonnes) reduced the increase in payload.

These muted grumbles went on for a few months, and then they stopped. Of course, persuading MPs to sanction another increase so soon after 38 tonnes was out of the question. So the freight directorate came up with an administrative sleight of hand, which gave the road lobby 40 tonnes, without the need to return to Parliament.

Overweight lorries face two types of penalty. The first is a fine. The second is a prohibition order, which means that part of the load has to be unloaded before the lorry can continue its journey.

In October 1983 the Department of Transport changed its rules. The reason for this change, as given in a circular to county councils and chief constables, was 'tightening . . . of manpower and financial budgets' – although Howell had promised an increase in enforcement when he introduced 38-tonners.[65]

Under the new rules lorries had to be 5 per cent overweight before they faced a prohibition notice, and 10 per cent overweight before they were liable to prosecution. In its circular, the department asked councils and the police to 'adopt similar practices . . . in the interest of uniformity of enforcement of lorry weight restrictions'.[66]

So the maximum weight of lorries that can now run on Britain's roads, without fear of any penalty, is 39.9 tonnes.

8 Restraining traffic

Road humps save lives by slowing up traffic. The concept is simple. A four-inch bump in the road forces traffic in residential areas to slow up, and comply with the 30 mph speed limit. The result is a sharp drop in the number of people killed on the roads.

But Britain lags behind most of the western world in introducing these life-saving measures, largely because of a highly effective rearguard action mounted by the road lobby and its road engineering allies.

'Speed kills' is a truism. Vulnerable road users, such as pedestrians and cyclists, can easily be killed by speeding vehicles. As a rule of thumb the threshold is a speed, at the time of collision, of 20 mph. For pedestrians a collision speed above 20 mph is a little bit like playing Russian roulette, with a bullet in every chamber. Below this speed, the chances of a pedestrian surviving an accident increase sharply.

In 1982 a West German government study showed that cutting the speed limit from just over 30 mph to slightly under 20 mph could cut road deaths by half. Researchers in countries as far apart as Sweden, the Netherlands and Japan have found that lower speeds save lives.[1] In Britain the lowest speed limit is 30 mph.

Even this limit is widely flouted. Most roads in Britain's built up areas have a 30 mph speed limit. Roughly 55 per cent of the country's road deaths occur on these roads. Many victims are pedestrians, often elderly people or children. Britain has a poor record for pedestrian safety, in comparison to its safety record for motorists, which is quite good.[2] And Britain's child safety record is appalling. A British child is twice as likely to die on the roads as one in the Netherlands, and three times as likely as one in Sweden.[3]

A road hump is a simple solution to the problem of the speeding motorist because it is self-enforcing. The British design of road hump is uncomfortable, but not dangerous, to drive over at more than 30 mph.

16 Road humps save lives – but Britain only has a handful of them

Europe took the lead in introducing road humps. In 1974, the Netherlands introduced an even more radical concept of *woonerven*.[4] This is a comprehensive package for streets in residential areas. It includes road humps, as well as other features designed to reduce vehicles' speeds. They included pinch points, where a narrowing road forces traffic to slow down, and cobbles. These schemes have been extremely successful and widely copied. One such scheme in Charlottenburg, a suburb of Berlin, which was introduced in 1982 cut the number of road accidents by two-thirds.[5]

But while Europe races ahead, Britain is still struggling to introduce one stage, road humps. In 1974, after a long campaign, the law was changed to allow road humps to be introduced experimentally. The government's Transport and Road Research Laboratory monitored several of these experiments and concluded that 'on the whole humps do reduce road accidents', as a laboratory spokesman cautiously put it.[6]

Local councils began to recognise the virtues of humps, and installed a few. But the legislation was ludicrous. Under the 1974 law, humps could only be installed as an experiment, for one year, so that even if councils had a hump that was working well, and saving lives, it had to be taken out after one year.

In 1978 the government consulted organisations about legislation to make permanent humps legal in Britain. The road lobby was consulted, as were the main local authority associations. But several environmental groups do not seem to have been consulted.[7]

The RAC continued to oppose the introduction of humps. The AA moderated its opposition, retreating to a position of conceding the principle, but making humps as difficult to install as possible.[8] It told the Department of Transport that the government would have to control strictly the design of the humps, and the circumstances where they might be used.

In 1980, Parliament passed a law making permanent road humps legal. All the department had to do was to make regulations governing the design and siting of humps. The department consulted. The regulations were not made until 1983. They followed the spirit of the AA's political line very closely indeed.

The details of the regulations had largely been decided by the department's road safety division, and the engineering advisers of the Association of Metropolitan Authorities, which represents most of the larger city councils.

The regulations were strict to the point of being ludicrous. Humps were outlawed close to bridges, bus stops, level crossings, the crest of a hill and within 50 metres of a zebra crossing – just in case they slowed traffic. One of the few places that humps could obviously and easily be installed was within 30 metres of a dead end, just in case anyone was tempted to exceed the speed limit in a cul de sac. The RAC characteristically greeted the new regulations by warning of the danger of road humps – to motorists.[9]

The regulations had the intended effect. By 1984, twelve months after road humps had been legalised, none of the seven biggest urban areas in England had installed a hump. West Yorkshire, for example, had investigated fifty-eight possible sites. It was still studying the one remaining site.[10]

The regulations were clearly impossibly strict, as local councils rapidly realised. Pressure from local councils forced the government to relax the regulations. In 1986 the government consulted on new regulations. The major change was that humps can be sited on zebra crossings, so that pedestrians can walk across the hump. But humps are still not allowed on the approaches to zebra crossings.[11]

In the twelve years that Britain spent procrastinating over its first road humps, the Netherlands installed nearly 3,000 *woonerven*. Britain does not have one, although in 1985 it did begin installing a much watered down version of *woonerven* (to the point where anyone from the Netherlands would be hard pushed to recognise a similarity) in half a dozen sites. As an experiment.[12]

The story of road humps is one example of a wider attempt by the road lobby, and its allies, to minimise restrictions on traffic. Cars and lorries can be dangerous. They are often unpleasant neighbours. A natural reaction is to want to control their use more closely. It is this closer control which the road lobby is trying to prevent.

Speed has been a constant obsession with the road lobby ever since the red flag act was repealed. In 1965, a 70 mph national limit was introduced as an experiment. The road lobby opposed the limit. The BRF wrote to Barbara Castle, then Minister of Transport, expressing 'serious doubts about the consequences of a blanket speed limit' and demanding the 'plainest possible evidence' before the limit was made permanent.[13] However, Castle was a strong enough minister to override the road lobby and she made the limit permanent.

By 1973, the AA was calling for the limit to be raised to 90 mph.[14] But events overtook the speedsters. The oil crisis, in 1973–4, forced the government to reduce speed limits to a maximum of 50 mph. By 1974, the AA and the RAC were calling for a 70 mph limit to be restored.[15] The limit was increased to 70 mph on motorways, later that year, and 60 mph on dual carriageways. In 1977, after further pressure from the road lobby, speed limits on dual carriageways were also raised to 70 mph, while the limit on other roads was also increased by 10 mph to 60 mph.

Another attempt to raise speed limits generally was made in 1984. This time the initiative came from Nicholas Ridley, the Secretary of State for Transport. Predictably, the AA and the RAC backed high speeds.[16] Equally predictable was the opposition of environmentalists. But the evidence that higher speeds would increase the number of accidents was overwhelming, and few in the department were prepared to back the Transport Secretary's line.

The motor industry's desire for high speeds stems partly from its need to export cars to countries which allow higher speeds, such as West Germany. But rather more important is its perception of speed as being a good selling point. The adverts for the Ford Granada in 1986 proclaimed its ability to reach a maximum speed of 111 mph. The Rover Sterling, one of the Rover 800 series, which was introduced in 1986, is 'first and foremost a car to be driven'. The copy burbles on that the engine has twenty-four valves 'generating full-blooded power that will take you over 130 mph before you know it'.[17] – an impressive contribution to European Road Safety Year.

The motor industry is equally keen to frustrate other restrictions on the use of cars and lorries. The most significant battles take place over plans to ban traffic from roads, or even over wider areas. The SMMT, for example, joined the FTA and the RHA in opposing the GLC's ban on lorries in London. This opposition had a long tradition. As long ago as 1920, the SMMT successfully prevented lorries from being banned on unsuitable roads in Cumberland.[18]

The basic motive for this opposition is that any restriction on traffic could affect sales of cars or lorries. Thus in 1979 road lobby groups in the Midlands opposed the government's plans to ration off-street car parking (an attempt to cut car traffic in congested city centres) because it could reduce car sales by 20 per cent.[19] Though doubtless there was an element of scaremongering in this claim, the fear was real enough. If restrictions on traffic make the car or lorry less useful, sales are bound to drop off to some extent.

Any restrictions on cars automatically enrage the RAC. The wrath of the lorry operators is guaranteed to fall on anyone who tries to restrict lorries. But any successful scheme which reduces traffic in urban areas also has its knock-on effect for the road builders. By far the best argument for building roads is the length of traffic jams. So reducing the queues in London, for example, would weaken the case for new roads enormously.

However, the presentation of the case against traffic restraint normally relies on the absolute and unqualified freedom of motorists to use the roads. The steering group to the Buchanan report described the car as:

> one of our most treasured possessions, or dearest ambitions, an immense convenience, an expander of the dimensions of life, an instrument of emancipation, a symbol of the modern age. To refuse to accept the challenge it presents would be an act of defeatism.[20]

Nicholas Ridley, who was later to become Transport Secretary, in 1977 presented a vision of absolute freedom:

> The private motorist . . . wants the independence and status of his motor car. He wants the chance to live a life that gives him a new dimension of freedom – freedom to go where he wants, when he wants, and for as long as he wants.[21]

Moves to restrict traffic on any scale became important only in the 1970s. The first big test came with the 'zone and collar' traffic experiment in Nottingham. The city had already pedestrianised its centre, causing the number of accidents there to drop by one-third. It then embarked on a much more ambitious plan to restrict traffic penetrating the town, beyond the main bypass.

The city threw a cordon around this bypass. Traffic signals controlled the flow of traffic into the city centre. As an alternative, motorists were encouraged to leave their cars in special car parks, and to take coaches into the centre. The coaches were given priority over cars at the traffic lights, and so did not suffer any delay.[22]

The idea had its technical problems, the biggest of which was that the experimental scheme had a cordon stretching round only one-third of the city. Motorists could drive round the cordon, although some chose to jump the lights instead.

But the chief problem was political. The RAC was active in opposing the scheme. It circulated local members asking them to protest. The two suburbs affected by the experiment were very different in character. One was mostly council housing, where few people had cars. The other suburb, one-tenth the size of the council estate, was mostly private housing, where many people had cars. Virtually all the complaints about the plan came from this smaller suburb.[23]

The Nottingham experiment started in August 1975, but was abandoned the next year. The RAC said that the city's traffic problems were not serious enough to justify such a radical scheme.[24] In the same year, a plan to introduce tolls for cars entering Bristol was also dropped because of opposition from the road lobby.

The problems were certainly much more serious in London. The Labour-controlled GLC had just abandoned the ringways. It was now groping towards an alternative policy to road building. It investigated a scheme for supplementing licensing under which motorists would pay for a licence (costing about £1.25 a day) to enter central London. The AA and the RAC again opposed the plan.[25]

The RAC correctly saw the plan as a clash of philosophies. It contrasted the GLC's plans to charge motorists with its proposals for 'constructive measures', which it defined as being new ring roads. It distributed thousands of leaflets putting its point of view.[26]

The decisive argument, from the GLC's point of view, was that any charge would bear most heavily on the poorest motorist – who were also likely to be Labour voters. In July 1975, the GLC decided to abandon its plans for supplementary licensing. Jim Daly, who chaired the GLC's transport committee, conceded in a letter to the RAC that 'any method of road pricing which gives the wealthy and the company car driver an advantage over the ordinary working man is socially unacceptable'.[27]

In 1977, the GLC tried a different tack, by introducing a 'no car' lane in Balham. The lane was open to buses, bicycles and lorries – but not cars. The attempt to drive a wedge between the different factions of the road lobby failed. The AA and the RAC were vocal in their opposition,[28] while the FTA and the RHA said nothing. The lane was installed weeks before the GLC election, which the Conservatives won. It was removed within weeks of this victory.

By 1981, Labour was back in control of the GLC. In 1984 the GLC introduced a right turn in Talgarth Road. Behind this seemingly innocuous measure was a grander design, which once again brought the road lobby into conflict with the GLC.

Talgarth Road is at the eastern end of the Hammersmith Flyover, the route of the A4 into central London. The right turn often blocked off one of the three lanes that carry the morning flood of traffic into central London, thus reducing the carrying capacity of the road by up to a third. The GLC had plans for a similar series of pinch points on the roads leading to central London, which by reducing the volume of traffic reaching the centre would free the centre of traffic jams.

The road lobby was incensed by the scheme, and suspected grander design. The AA accused the GLC of 'mischievous ideology' and was able to enlist the support of Conservative backbenchers. Within three days of the scheme's introduction, ministers joined the road lobby chorus, with Lynda Chalker asking the GLC to take the scheme out.[29]

In the face of this opposition the GLC did modify its stance, reducing the squeeze on traffic into central London but keeping the right turn. This provoked a further warning from Nicholas Ridley, who was deeply opposed to the GLC, both for party political reasons and because of his transport politics. Calling the plan 'a nonsense', Ridley said it was 'a matter of grave concern to motorists in west London . . . I hope you will reconsider this and restore the necessary capacity to the road forthwith'.[30] The GLC did not agree and Talgarth Road still had its right turn several months after the GLC was abolished – although the road lobby had effectively caused the GLC to abandon its plans for other pinch points.

Meanwhile the road lobby has been equally keen to oppose any plans to ban lorries, although with markedly less success than its opposition to bans on cars.

The Labour GLC of 1973 to 1977 flirted with a lorry ban. But the GLC's officers persuaded councillors to set up a conference to talk about ways of reducing the environmental nuisance of lorries. And the conference talked, and talked, until the Conservatives were elected in 1977 when the political enthusiasm for any ban disappeared.

The next round of the fight to restrict lorries was fought at the unlikely battleground of Windsor. The political problem for lorry operators is that although they are naturally close to the Conservative Party, it is Conservative voters that often bear the brunt of lorry traffic.

In 1978, the Conservative-controlled Berkshire County Council approved a six-month experimental ban on a short stretch of road in Windsor. This effectively banned heavy lorries from the entire town. The FTA and the RHA, backed by the National Farmers' Union, took Berkshire to court to try and block the ban. This was a test case. The operators' intention, as their counsel freely conceded in court, was to warn off other local authorities considering a similar ban.[31] But the operators, who were demanding a public inquiry into the scheme, lost their case. Berkshire, ironically a member of the FTA, went ahead with the ban.

Back in London, Labour won the GLC elections in 1981. One of the main planks of the party's election platform was to study a ban on heavy lorries. It set up a committee of inquiry, under a lawyer, Derek Wood, QC.

There was a long wrangle over the membership of the inquiry, which all sides calculated would be rather more important than any evidence which it heard. The GLC wanted a limited number of people on the committee. The environmentalists (and particularly groups such as Friends of the Earth, the London Amenity and Transport Association and Transport 2000) had built up good links with the GLC. The GLC had little sympathy with the vested interests of the road lobby, which it saw as being dedicated to opposing any progress.

It was exactly the same fight that has taken place over the composition of every other official inquiry, with one important difference. This time it was the environmentalists that held the inside track with officialdom, and were able to capitalise on this advantage.

Even so, the lorry operators managed to persuade the GLC to put their representatives, one from retail distributors and the other jointly representing the FTA and the RHA, on the committee, even if the membership was not as tilted in their favour as they would normally like it to be.

The inquiry did not report until 1983. It favoured a ban on heavy lorries (over 16 tonnes) in London, although the two representatives of the lorry operators dissented from the majority report. However, the committee unanimously concluded that a ban on heavy lorries at night and during the weekend would 'give significant relief to those living on or near the major lorry routes of London' but would have 'serious implications for only a small minority of firms'.[32]

The road lobby immediately mounted a campaign against the ban, with the CBI, the SMMT and the BRF's group, Movement for

London, joining forces with the FTA and the RHA.[33] The cost of a ban was variously quoted as being £250 million a year or £750 million a year, while the CBI claimed that it would cost one company alone £60 million.[34] The publicity emphasised that 'London needs Lorries' a point that was driven home by handouts picturing a small, two-axle lorry, which caused some mirth at the GLC, which was trying to ban only much heavier articulated lorries.[35]

The FTA tried a gentle, but transparent, approach, offering to help the GLC solve its lorry problem – in the hope of forestalling a ban.[36]

However, by 1983 the GLC was facing abolition. It decided that the weight of opposition to an all-out ban was too great for it to make any progress before it was abolished. It opted instead for a partial lorry ban, at nights and over the weekend.[37]

The road lobby was also forced to change tack, arguing that the costs of this partial ban would be enormous and that the environmental gain would be negligible. The FTA, in particular, argued that this partial ban would have no environmental gain and that the cost of the ban would be enormous. And with the forthcoming abolition of the GLC firmly in mind, it called for a public inquiry – which would inevitably delay any ban until after abolition.

The FTA mounted an effective local campaign, persuading its members to write to the GLC to object (860 firms did), and lobbied local councillors. But it had little success.

The road lobby had much greater success with their allies in the Department of Transport, and Nicholas Ridley, the Secretary of State. In response to the GLC's consultation, Ridley criticised the GLC for not heeding the views of industry and commerce and called for a public inquiry. He said that the Wood report had not been unanimous and that two members of the committee had dissented, and 'explained why they thought the cost to industry of a night and weekend ban would be far greater than those assumed by other members'.[38]

Ridley was wrong. The Wood committee was unanimous in its conclusion about a night and weekend ban. The note of dissent only referred to a full-scale ban.

The GLC decided to go ahead with a ban, without a public inquiry. Ridley immediately decided, even before the GLC's committee meeting had finished, to order the GLC to have a public inquiry.[39] The GLC took Ridley to court, arguing that it had already held a public inquiry (although this was not the statutory inquiry demanded by Ridley), and had also consulted widely and that there was no need for yet another inquiry. The court agreed, and ruled against Ridley. The ban was introduced at the beginning of 1986, just weeks before the GLC was abolished.

17 *Sam Toy, president of the SMMT, 1985–6, and until 1986 chairman and managing director of Ford of Great Britain*

18 *Peter Witt, the BRF's director*

9 Buses, trains and the road lobby

Twenty-five years ago, Britain's railways faced a grim future. Their losses were mounting. They were losing traffic to the new motorways. Publicly the road lobby largely stood aloof from the railways' misfortunes. Privately it was delighted, and quite willing to assist the railways over the abyss.

The railways were the road lobby's traditional enemies, dating back to the foundation of the BRF in 1932. Before the war the BRF repeatedly called for 'the general closing down of branch lines and of intermediate main line stations'[1] arguing:

> Had road transport existed when the railways were built, very few of their branch lines and wayside stations would ever have come into being. The functions of these would have been filled by roads. They should be filled by roads today. These branch lines and wayside stations eat up a disproportionate amount of the railways' revenue.[2]

By the 1950s, the road lobby had toned down its public pronouncements. In 1959, the Conservative Party described in the road haulage press as 'the answer to the hauliers' prayer' won the general election. The new Minister of Transport, Ernest Marples, decided to set up an inquiry into the railways, to study ways of cutting costs. A junior minister told the RHA's annual dinner that the inquiry 'will commend itself to those present at this dinner'. The RHA, as the minister was pleased to note, 'was not slow to put . . . its views about the railways'. It wanted lines closed, so as to divert freight onto the roads.[3]

The inquiry was inconclusive, and its report was concerned largely with recommending improvements to the railways' management. But Marples selected one of the inquiry's team, Richard Beeching, to draw up a cost-cutting plan.[4]

The Beeching report proposed ripping up one-third of the railway network.[5] It provoked an extremely hostile public reaction. *The Times*

19 The road lobby's lavish publicity material

carried a whole page of letters on the subject, few of which supported Beeching. But the road lobby kept out of this public debate.

In the House of Commons, the debate on the Beeching report lasted two days. The Labour Party opposed the cuts. (Although Bob Mellish, an MP sponsored by the Transport and General Workers' Union, made an embarrassing plea for greater road investment and admitted 'certain lines . . . are uneconomic. At the end of the day some of these lines may have to be closed'.[6]

Two MPs representing bus interests spoke in favour of the report, doubtless because the bus industry hoped to pick up some extra passengers if railways were closed.

The road lobby MPs adopted guerilla tactics, and concentrated on heckling MPs such as Jeremy Thorpe who spoke against the report. In one intervention Roger Gresham Cooke, formerly the BRF's chief executive, said that Beeching 'may be optimistic about the profits . . . but does not that make the case even stronger for going even further than Dr Beeching proposes'.[7]

The most frequent interruptions came from Geoffrey Wilson, who was the Conservative chairman of the All Party Road Study Group. Eventually Wilson's tactics so exasperated MPs that there was a general cry of 'sit down'.[8]

By the mid–1960s, the Beeching cuts were in full swing. Hundreds of miles of railway were closed every year, despite the election of a Labour government in 1964. The main source of pressure for closures came from the civil service, both from the ministry and the Treasury, which saw the cuts as a way of saving money. The pressure groups of the road lobby played no part in urging individual closures. Paradoxically, British Rail was active in supporting closures, which it saw as being a test of its management ability.

In 1967, Barbara Castle introduced a new Transport Bill, an attempt to stabilise the balance between road and rail. The two main proposals in the bill were to introduce a system of subsidies for the railways and a system of quantity licensing for road freight, to divert freight from road to rail, and specifically aimed at large loads travelling over long distances.

The road lobby's response was ferocious. It set up a special group, the Transport Users' Joint Committee, to fight the bill and the RHA launched a coordinated campaign with Aims of Industry. It was virtually an action replay of the campaign against the 1947 Transport Act.[9]

Most of the opposition centred around the proposals to license lorries. Whole-page adverts were placed in the national press claiming that 'food bills will go up by an unnecessary £16 million'.[10] Peter Walker, the Conservatives' transport spokesman, said that the bill was designed to 'prop up an ailing railway system by artificial means and at the expense of basically more efficient road services'[11]

However, the BRF also opposed 'the principle of subsidies. Its view has always been that users of transport should bear the cost of the services they use'.[12]

The Conservative Party cooperated closely with the road lobby in opposing the legislation. Peter Walker paid £10,000 out of his own pocket to set up a research group to provide arguments against the bill.[13]

In the main debate on the bill in the House of Commons, Enoch Powell, speaking from the opposition front bench, underlined the link with the road lobby. 'As the BRF says there would be no point in the relevant proposals in this bill unless it was the intention to force trade and industry to use rail transport . . .'[14]

By the third week in January, the bill had attracted 2,000 amendments, and the total eventually rose to 2,500 – two and a half times as many amendments as the 1947 Transport Bill had attracted. The committee considering this bill (and the amendments) met for a record forty-five sittings.[15]

The bill became law in 1968. The railways got their subsidy. But although the quantity licensing proposals came through this attack almost unscathed, they were never brought into force because of the opposition of the Transport and General Workers' Union. 'Frank Cousins' socialism stops dead at the door of a lorry', as Barbara Castle acidly remarked.[16]

However, the legislation did slow down the rate of railway closures, which by the early 1970s had virtually ground to a halt. But the size of British Rail's subsidy (which was small by European standards)[17] was coming under increasing pressure, chiefly from the anti-railway element in the Ministry and civil servants in the Treasury, who had tried to stop subsidies being included in the 1968 act in the first place.[18]

But the attempt to start a fresh round of railway cuts backfired when the plans were leaked to the *Sunday Times*, in 1972.[19] In the 1960s the railway interests failed to capitalise on the public support they had. The railway management had been effectively neutralised as a political force by nationalisation.

The railway unions' main strategy was to seek TUC support for a campaign against closures. But the TUC would not support the railway unions because of the opposition of the Transport and General Workers' Union. Consequently the union's campaign strategy collapsed.

A number of grass roots pressure groups were also set up to oppose closures. A few of the groups set up to save individual lines were successful.[20] But the national groups were poorly financed, had neither full-time staff nor offices (apart from the front rooms of supporters) and had a negligible effect on policy.[21]

This time the railway unions managed to harness public support. They entered an alliance with a number of environmental groups, and set up a new pro-public transport pressure group, Transport 2000, as a counterweight to the road lobby.[22]

The government backtracked in the face of this public outcry, and rethought its policy. Its next piece of legislation on the subject, the 1974 Railways Act, was a complete 'U-turn' which, instead of cutting the railway subsidy, ensured its future.

The road lobby was dismayed by this turn of events. It saw the railway subsidy as money that was being wasted when it could be gainfully invested in new roads. The FTA said it raised 'the spectre of an unholy alliance between British environmentalists and the continental pro-rail philosophy'.[23] The environmentalists, on the other hand, saw the railway subsidy as being the cornerstone of a new philosophy for transport, an alternative to motorways and juggernauts.

Meanwhile the road lobby was also under attack from its own fringes. The Railway Conversion League, a group with a worldwide membership of forty-three (in 1984),[24] which believes that railways ought to be converted into roads, attacked the road lobby for 'the present policy of appeasement'.

The BRF retorted:

> We cannot agree with the extreme and extravagant views of the Railway Conversion League . . . a doctrinaire roads-only attitude is as out of date as the trendier no more roads and rail only cries from fringe groups.[25]

In 1974, the BRF decided to take a stronger line against subsidies – for buses as well as trains. In a letter to the leaders of political parties, the BRF complained about the subsidy to British Rail and the likelihood that the new transport supplementary grant system being introduced would mean an increase in subsidies generally. 'These decision are basically not transport decisions . . . They are, in effect, welfare decisions and probably very inefficient ones at that'.[26]

By 1976, the BRF was becoming much more strident in its attacks on the railways' subsidy, and calling for a 'serious' study of converting railways into roads.

'All of us have been having the wool pulled over our eyes by a campaign of misstatement and outright deception by the railway unions and their supporters', said the BRF's chairman, Tony de Boer. He called on environment secretary Tony Crosland to face up to 'the relentless campaign of scaremongering waged by the rail unions'.[27]

In its response to the green paper on transport policy, the BRF concentrated its fire on the railway and bus subsidy. 'The government must end support for loss-making transport services and inject the capital resources into roads.' In addition to its appeals for a cut in subsidy, the BRF also wanted British Rail to drop its plans for high-speed trains.[28]

Although the main thrust of this attack was clearly aimed at rail subsidies, in private it was also concerned to reduce bus subsidies. By

1976 these were almost as large as the subsidy to rail passengers. It was a delicate political balancing act.

The road lobby has never had any doubt what the choice would be, if it were ever forced to choose between buses and its policy. In 1962, the Roads Campaign Council was actively lobbying for more parking in city centres. The bus operators objected, on the grounds that this was an exclusively pro-motorist policy and would do nothing to help buses. The man from the SMMT was brutal, but to the point. How much, he enquired, did the bus operators pay towards the Roads Campaign Council? Nothing, was the reply. And the council moved on to its next business.[29]

Nonetheless, the BRF wanted to reduce subsidies, and keep its bus industry allies, if at all possible. In October 1976, it met the new Secretary of State for Transport, Bill Rodgers. Rodgers listened to the BRF's complaints about soaring subsidies and asked the group for a paper on the subject. It argued that roads 'compete with subsidies for part of the transport budget' and complained of a shift from road spending 'which by next year will have fallen by one-third towards public transport support, which has trebled'.

Under pressure to cut back on spending, Rodgers told the large city councils to cut their public transport subsidies. Two cities, London and Sheffield, had been pegging their fares by increasing their public transport subsidies. In London the council put up bus and tube fares. The GLC, which was Labour-controlled, together with the railway unions and the Transport and General Workers' Union (representing bus workers) launched a 'save our services' campaign to try to stave off cuts in services. But the campaign had only limited success.

Nevertheless it caused the BRF some angst, at least in part because it was then courting the transport workers' union to persuade it to back a campaign for higher spending on roads. However, the BRF decided not to try to oppose the campaign, although its London man did contact the opposition Conservatives on the GLC, who presumably needed little persuading to oppose this Labour initiative.

Despite these cuts, subsidies still came under attack, if not because they were diverting money from road building, because they were causing higher motoring taxes. Nicholas Ridley, while still a back-bench MP, complained: 'To go on ploughing money into public transport is to cause these high rates of petrol tax and road tax to find the money to pay subsidies.'[30]

The road lobby was also critical of attempts to electrify the railways, because money might be diverted from road building:

We object to the use of public money for schemes which pass no normal economic or financial test and are justified by vague and unquantified references to energy shortages, national security and the environment without any reference to the fact that resources for electrification will present a diversion from other areas of investment in the roads and transport budget.[31]

However, the election of a Conservative government in 1979, pledged to curb rail subsidies, caused the BRF to change tack abruptly. At the beginning of 1981, the BRF and British Rail jointly wrote to the transport secretary, Norman Fowler, asking for increased spending on 'infrastructure', a vogue word at the time which included spending on roads as well as railways. The submission, which was signed by the railway unions as well as other groups in the road lobby, called for greater spending on new roads as well as on electrification.[32]

It was a considerable coup for the road lobby, which had successfully gained the support of the major financial backers of Transport 2000, one of the BRF's major opponents. It had absolutely no effect on the plans for electrification, which remained stalled for another three years. But road spending continued to rise in real terms, as it had since the Tories were elected in 1979.[33]

In practical terms this 'unique collaborative initiative' achieved little. The Tories were committed to increasing road spending. And did. The Cabinet Office was committed to blocking railway electrification. There was nothing the combined road and rail lobbies could do about that.

For the next few months, the road lobby's views were muted, as the BRF decided to adopt a less adversarial approach.

However, fresh rail cuts had been mooted ever since the Conservatives were elected in 1979. In 1982, David Howell, the new Secretary of State for Transport, set up an inquiry into British Rail's finances. It was headed by Sir David Serpell, a former permanent secretary at the Department of Transport.[34]

Serpell's report produced a number of different options for reducing the railways' subsidy. The most extreme of these involved cutting back the 11,000-mile network to just 1,600 miles. News of the cutbacks began to filter out in the weeks before the report was published. Public reaction to the cuts was strong enough to panick Howell into ruling out this most extreme option.[35]

In the debate on the Serpell report, the Conservative chairman of the All Party Roads Study Group, Peter Fry, accused British Rail's 'dirty tricks' department of orchestrating the leaks. Fry complained that too many MPs wanted to bury 'Serpell rather than praising it'.

Fry was clearly not one of these: he went on to back Serpell's plan to replace local trains with buses.[36]

The BRF welcomed the Serpell report, and months after the event could happily fall into line and reject 'the more extreme options' while supporting 'the closure of the heaviest loss-making routes and their replacement by bus services'. It also gave some support to 'limited rail to road conversion', an issue which had been given a new outing round the political arena since the Tories came to power, although to no practical effect.[37]

The main focus of the BRF's efforts in these years was the transport supplementary grant. This grant, like the better-known rate support grant, is a system for central government to aid local council spending. The grant replaced the old system of giving fixed percentage grants to road schemes in 1975, and because of pressure from environmentalists, it was widened to include all forms of transport, and not just roads.

The way the grant worked was that councils would put up their spending plans to the department. If the department approved them, it paid the councils a proportion of the cost. What happened, not infrequently, was that councils would take government money for bus subsidies and switch it to road building. Or, and this is what annoyed the road lobby, some councils took money for roads and spent it on public transport.

The concern surfaced in 1982 when Sir Peter Baldwin, the department's chief civil servant, was giving evidence to the House of Commons transport committee. Peter Fry, a senior committee member, said that councils had been taking money for public transport 'out of what appeared to be capital project money . . . that has caused a lot of ill-feeling'.[38]

The road lobby's solution, which was dreamed up by the BRF's economist Andrew Street, was to limit the transport grant to capital spending. For most councils, this effectively meant restricting transport spending that had government support to roads. Very few councils have any sizeable public transport investment plans. The change would have meant creating a council fund which was supported by the government and which could be spent only on roads. Public transport would have to fight for its share of the council cake with all the other calls on spending, from police to sewers.

The BRF's line was backed by the county surveyors, the advisers to the Association of County Councils. When the change came, the department went even further than the BRF had wanted. The transport grant was, in 1986, not only limited to capital spending, but capital spending on roads.

10 The partial ministry

In the battle for heavier lorries and more motorways, the civil servants in the Department of Transport are firmly on the side of the road lobby. The clearest evidence of this bias is an internal minute, written by Joe Peeler, a senior civil servant.

Peeler advocated 'rigging' an inquiry by 'impartial people of repute' who would come to 'a sensible conclusion in line with the department's view'.[1]

The significance of this minute is first that Peeler is confident that his interpretation of the department's view will be shared by other senior civil servants. Indeed he spells it out. 'It is assumed that we wish . . . to move as soon as parliamentary and public opinion will let us to a maximum weight [for lorries] of 38 or 40 tons.'[2]

Peeler had every reason to be confident. He was an under-secretary, the third highest rank in the civil service. He sent his minute to Peter Lazarus, who was then a deputy secretary, the second highest rank. Lazarus then forwarded Peeler's minute to Sir Peter Baldwin, the permanent secretary and top civil servant, together with a three-page note of his own, which supported Peeler's general line, although in rather more diplomatic language.[3]

Secondly the minute shows that Peeler, as head of the department's freight directorate, viewed it as his job to promote the road haulage industry, both with its fight with the environmentalists over lorry weights and in disputes with the unions. He twice refers to the inquiry giving:

> an opportunity to the road haulage industry to improve both its public image and its organisational cohesiveness. . . . Ultimately such action on a combined basis could have wider consequences in other spheres, e.g. in producing far more unity and efficiency in dealing with pay matters.[4]

The civil servants are just as biased when it comes to building roads, as Barbara Castle found out when she became Minister of Transport

20 Sir Peter Baldwin, former permanent secretary at the Department of Transport – now on the AA's ruling committee

in 1965. She felt that the motorway programme was out of control. Castle discussed the problem with one of her more enlightened civil servants:

> He agreed with me when I said I had no effective control over the roads programme and that we had no machinery for integrating road strategy into our general transport policy. He agreed, too, that this strategy ought not to be in the hands of highway engineers.[5]

Castle was told that any necessary coordination of the road programme with general transport policy would be carried out by her permanent secretary, Thomas Padmore. She was unhappy with Padmore, and tried to have him moved, but failed after a press leak.[6] When Castle left the Ministry, the road strategy was still not subordinate to a more general transport policy, which was a source of complaint by environmentalists throughout the 1970s. After retiring from the civil service, Padmore joined the RAC's political lobbying arm, its public policy committee.[7]

A decade later, John Horam found the same structural problem when he became the minister in charge of roads. 'You had this feeling that there was a master plan', he said.[8]

The road engineers were a force apart in the department. They even had their own separate building, south of the river, and away from the main ministry building in Marsham Street, near Victoria, where ministers and most senior civil servants worked.

The chief highway engineer at the time was Ron Bridle, a large grey-bearded Welshman. Horam recalls: 'He seemed to me to have influence. There was a network of influence that was difficult to pin down. It was very pervasive.'[9]

Not only ministers are under pressure to conform to the department's view. One civil servant who joined the highways section at the end of the 1970s was told bluntly: 'If you don't believe in road building you shouldn't be in this job.'[10]

Roger Liddle, who was appointed as political adviser to Bill Rodgers and Horam in an attempt to provide an independent source of advice to the civil services, recalls an occasion when he was briefed about the railways. 'We had been talking about one hour. The civil servant looked at the clock and said: "That's £50,000 of public money that could have been spent on housing".'[11]

The reason for the department's bias is historical. Lloyd George had wanted to create a ministry of ways and communications, which would be in charge of both roads and railways. The road lobby feared that its interests would be subordinated to the railways. Under pressure from road lobby MPs, the bill was amended.

The Ministry of Transport was partly set up because, as a permanent secretary later put it, 'motorists and road interests were pressing for more funds to build better roads'.[12] Initially the ministry took direct control of the railways, raising road lobby fears, 'there were those who sensed a sinister encroachment by the railways'. But control of the railways ceased in 1923, two years after the ministry had been set up.[13]

From 1923 onwards, the ministry had an arms length relationship with the railways. But it had a much more direct interest in building roads, and the highest paid job in the ministry was the Director General of Roads. This continued to be one of the most important jobs in the ministry for nearly sixty years. The distinct position of Director General of Highways, then the second most important job in the Department of Transport, was not abolished until 1978.

The creation of the Ministry of Transport was one of the road lobby's greatest coups. The ministry has been more or less consistently pro-road throughout its existence and has provided the road lobby with a toehold in government.

In its early years, the ministry had so little to do that it was nearly abolished. But during the 1930s it acquired more responsibilities for road transport. Legislation passed in 1930 made the ministry responsible for licensing buses, followed by goods vehicles (1933), driving tests (1934) and major roads (1936). Each of these new responsibilities tied the ministry more closely to the wheels of road transport.

This balance did not change after the Second World War. Road transport was too firmly entrenched in the ministry. The nationalisation of the railways further reduced their political influence. The old company bosses had considerable personal sway with ministers.[14] But this disappeared once the British Transport Commission had been set up.

The motorway building programme further strengthened the grip of road transport in the ministry, particularly with the establishment of regional road construction units from 1968 onwards. Despite the abolition of these units in 1981, the internal balance in the ministry has barely changed in thirty years.

In 1986, according to official figures, the Department of Transport employed 12,500 civil servants to work on roads and road transport, seventy-two to work on railways and about fifty-three on public transport.[15]

These figures overstate the case. The road transport numbers include everyone from the chief highway engineer, who can have an important influence on policy, to the clerks at the driving licence centre at Swansea, who are unlikely to have much influence.

A more significant comparison is the number of staff at under-secretary level, because at this rank civil servants can have a considerable effect on policy. There is one under-secretary in charge of railway policy. Another is in charge of freight policy, in other words pushing for heavier lorries. A further eleven are concerned with road building or road transport.

The balance is important for two reasons. First, the weight of civil service advice will always lean towards road transport. Second, the sheer numerical imbalance means that the opportunities for promotion will invariably involve moves into sections of the ministry concerned with road transport, where even the independent-minded will find it difficult to avoid picking up some of the prevailing philosophy.

However, the department is not monolithic. Far from every civil servant is a rabid supporter of the road lobby. The divisions in the outside world are mirrored inside the department. Some civil servants are extremely pro-road. A few are extremely pro-rail, in a couple of instances to the point of being train spotters. Some are keen environmentalists. But the balance is overwhelmingly pro-road.

One of the most important tussles between factions in the department is, however, between the engineers and the economists. The economists are not environmentalists. They just want to make sure that the roads are worth building. The engineers want to be left alone to build their roads.

The main focus of this tussle is a technique known as cost benefit analysis. This was originally developed for roads in Britain in the 1950s, as a way of convincing the Treasury that it was worth investing money in roads. It now takes the form of a computer program, COBA. In essence, COBA compares the cost of the road with the money value of the time that motorists will save by using the new road.

COBA is difficult to justify intellectually. But it was given a clean bill of health by a committee, headed by Sir George Leitch, which was set up in 1977 to investigate the department's methods of justifying roads.[16] This committee decided that COBA was worth keeping because it was the major curb on the wilder excesses of the engineers.

But engineers can get round a poor COBA. The North Devon Link Road was notorious for having a poor COBA. In COBA, a positive result probably means that a road is worth investing in. A negative result means that the road is not worth building. Under Rodgers and Horam, progress on the road was stalled, because it was such poor value for money. It was finally approved in 1981.

Part of the reason for the Department of Transport's bias towards the road lobby is that the lobbyists and the civil servants come from similar backgrounds, and maybe even the same school. Both are overwhelmingly male and middle class. At the top end of the scale they may frequent the same clubs. And almost without exception they share the seemingly trivial details of social conditioning – a car, a house with a garden in the suburbs – that are so important in prejudicing attitudes to transport policy.

To a man driving into work from the suburbs the biggest problem is the traffic jams that hold him up on his way to work. The solution to this problem does not require any thought. A new, wider road will obviously speed up traffic. It is this knee-jerk reaction which is the main argument for building roads in urban areas.

The woman standing at the bus stop in the driving rain naturally has a different perspective on what is wrong with transport policy. But for the men driving past in their cars her problem, for the most part, is beyond their understanding.

While civil servants often have a good relationship with the road lobbyists, their relations with environmental groups are often more strained. Partly this is the result of an age gap between the two groups. The environmentalists are often young, and full of youthful enthusiasm. They have to be to work for the pittance they are paid. The civil servants, on the other hand, find some of the environmentalists' ideas threaten their lifestyle, and anyway have a natural resistance to new and radical ideas.

This gulf is closing. Friends of the Earth, for instance, was virtually banned from the department for the first six years of its existence. Now it is as welcome as the road lobby. Its views, however, are by no means as welcome.

The closeness between the road lobby and the civil service is illustrated by the number of civil servants who take up positions in the road lobby on retiring.

It is far from unknown for civil servants to join pressure groups when they retire. One academic study turned up seventeen examples.[17] But most joined pressure groups with no direct interest in their previous official work. Only one example (Chris Hall) worked for the Ministry of Transport. Ironically, he went to work for an environmental group: the Ramblers' Association.

What is quite stunning is the frequency with which ministry men turn up in the road lobby, a few months later, almost as if it was a natural avenue of progress. Five of the eight most senior engineers in the ministry went on to work for or advise the road lobby. For the first fifty years of the ministry's existence, there was at least one, and normally more than one, former senior engineer working for the road lobby (or advising it). Each one of these men would be in a powerful position to influence the ministry's senior engineer, who would have been a junior engineer in the days when he held the top job.

Two of the prewar engineers, Sir Henry Maybury and John Killick, became active in the road lobby after retiring. The process reached a peak in the 1950s. Lyddon was the chief roads engineer from 1942 to 1945. After retiring he went on to run the Asphalt Roads Association, and he was active in the BRF during the 1950s. His successor was his deputy, Major Hubert Aldington. He left in 1949, and joined the board of the Amalgamated Roadstone Corporation, one of the more important road building firms, as well as becoming an adviser to the BRF, a position he held until 1965. Allan Baker became chief road engineer in 1954, retiring nine years later in 1963. From 1965 to 1969 he was a consultant to the AA.[18]

In more recent times, five permanent secretaries at the ministry have taken an interest in the road lobby after their retirement. Sir Leonard Browett left the ministry to go to work for the National Union of Manufacturers (now part of the CBI). In the 1950s, he led BRF delegations to the ministry to lobby for higher lorry speed limits and heavier weights.

Sir Cyril Birtchnell became active in the RAC in the early 1960s, while Sir Thomas Padmore, who Barbara Castle clashed with, was active in the RAC's public policy committee after his retirement from the early 1970s into the 1980s. The RAC's public policy committee also picked up Sir John Garlick, a former permanent secretary at the Department of the Environment in the days when that department controlled the transport ministry, as a replacement for Padmore. Sir Peter Baldwin, who was permanent secretary of the Department of Transport until 1983, subsequently joined the AA's committee.

Apart from this run of chief roads engineers and permanent secretaries at least four other ministry civil servants have gone on to positions in the road lobby.[19]

One of the more remarkable of these links was William Glanville, who was head of the Road Research Laboratory from 1939 to 1965. Glanville did not just become active in the road lobby after he retired, but he was on the RAC's public policy committee for twelve years before he retired.[20]

The Road Research Laboratory was extremely pro-road during these early years. It was the road lobby's idea in the first place to set up a laboratory. In the mid 1950s, one county surveyor put it this way: 'we pick-and-shovel engineers are proud of our connections with the Road Research Laboratory and regard it very much as our own private body'.[21]

Another of the more notable links is Sir Alex Samuels, who chaired an official committee on London's traffic in the 1950s and who was Barbara Castle's adviser on traffic in the late 1960s. By the mid 1970s, he was chairing the BRF's London group, Movement for London.

County surveyors have always had close links with the road lobby. Since 1970, at least four county surveyors have become active in the road lobby. The staunchest supporters of the motorway programme, Maynard Lovell and James Drake, both formed links with the BRF. Lovell chaired the BRF's group in the south-west.[22] When Drake retired as head of the ministry's north-west road construction unit he became a director of Leonard Fairclough, the road builders. He represented the firm on the BRF's council until 1979.[23]

Civil servants rarely parade their views in public. But on the odd occasions that they do, they reveal a clear commitment. In 1973, Leonard Mills, the deputy director of highways, told a conference in Southampton:

> Now there is a growing body of opinion that roads are causing irreparable damage to the environment . . . I believe this is a mistaken view, that in fact more harm will be done by not making proper provision for the motor car and that new roads are necessary for the improvement of the living standards of the larger part of the population. Inadequate communications, resulting in higher costs for food and other goods and in reduced opportunities

for social mobility, affect everyone and particularly those on low incomes.[24]

Thirteen years on, these views have barely changed among the senior staff in the department. Sir Peter Lazarus succeeded Baldwin as permanent secretary, and retired in 1986. Speaking shortly after he retired, Lazarus called for an increase in road spending: 'The problem area that I have identified is highways where in addition to all the planning problems, the resources are too limited.'

Lazarus said that road spending should not count as public expenditure.

> We cannot afford not to spend adequately on our roads. But if there is continuing pressure to keep public expenditure under control and if all expenditure on roads infrastructure is to continue to count as public expenditure then the claims of roads, as against health service, education, the elderly and defence will never be adequately met.[25]

One of the most common complaints about road inquiries during the 1970s was that they were rigged. The road was being promoted by the ministry. The inspector was appointed by the ministry, which took the final decision. The ministry was judge in its own cause.

It was not a new point. As far back as 1952, Lord Llewellin described an occasion when he appeared at a public inquiry on behalf of Middlesex County Council, which wanted to build a road. He asked about the attitude of the Ministry of Transport to the scheme and was told 'it is their plan. It is their project. They are paying about 90 per cent of the cost'. Llewellin remarked: 'I do not suppose we shall have much trouble before this inspector from the Ministry of Transport.' And he did not.[26]

The official files for this period now shed some light on how ministry inspectors were appointed. One official minuted:

> You will no doubt be aware that A.H. Dodd, the divisional road engineer at Manchester, is retired ... at his request and with a strong recommendation from Hugh-Jones [the ministry's chief roads engineer] we have added his name to our panel of persons suitable to hold public inquiries on behalf of the minister.[27]

Although the government did have an internal committee on public inquiries, presided over by a treasury official, appropriately called Playfair, the inspectors were anything but independent. In 1953, the ministry had sixteen inspectors. Seven of them were former Ministry of Transport officials, and three of these were retired roads engineers.[28] The practice was strikingly different in Scotland, where most inspectors had a legal background.

Despite an inquiry procedure heavily weighted in its favour, the ministry still ran into trouble at inquiries. One occasion was an inquiry into a section of the M5, in 1949.

It was a remarkable inquiry, not in the least because it was held before the ministry had the legal power to build motorways. It was a process referred to in the inquiry as 'sterilising' – making sure that land was available for a road.

One of the ministry's divisional road engineers, J.E. Cardell, was cross-examined by a lawyer representing local landowners. The lawyer wanted to know how much the road was going to cost and when it was going to be built.

Cardell appealed to the inspector for help, in the face of this aggressive (as he saw it) questioning. He said it was not his job to justify the decision to build the road and asked the inspector to protect him from this line of questioning. The inspector declined to help him out.[29]

Cardell sent off a furious minute to London, complaining about the inspector. 'I did not get any support from the inspector when I appealed to him . . . he did not effectively support me.'

As the result of this minute, the ministry tightened up its rules for inspectors. The circular which guided inspectors on how to conduct public inquiries was changed to tell inspectors not to allow engineers to be cross-examined.

Inspectors continued to be appointed by the ministry until 1976, when to try to head off some of the criticism the job of picking inspectors was transferred to the Lord Chancellor's office. In practice, all that happened was that the civil servant who did the picking, Mary Burr, transferred her files from the ministry to the Lord Chancellor's office.[30]

Despite their careful selection, one or two inspectors have broken ranks. But the ministry has evolved an elaborate structure to make sure that a dissident inspector's views have as little weight as possible, and also to make sure that the embarrassment is not repeated.

One of these dissidents was Hugh Gardner, a former agriculture ministry civil servant. Gardner presided over an inquiry into one part of the M42, in the Midlands, in 1976. The opposition argued that the road was not necessary. Gardner's report, which was published in 1978, did not quite go that far, but said that 'no further contracts should be let until there has been a public discussion of the need for the M42'.[31]

But what really got up the department's nose was criticism of it for its 'mother knows best' attitude. From 1976 to 1979, Gardner did not get another inquiry until this curious oversight was brought to the notice of Bill Rodgers. Rodgers asked why this inspector was not getting any more inquiries. Gardner was promptly given another inquiry.

Apart from punishing dissident inspectors, the main strategy is to water down any criticism systematically.

After an inspector has written an inquiry report it is sent to the department's local director, the person who was in charge of proposing the scheme in the first place. The report, together with the director's recommendation, is then forwarded to the regional director, one of the seven under-secretaries employed by the department at its regional offices.

This regional director 'having regard to the weight and nature of the objections . . . may personally decide to approve the making of the order'. In cases where the regional director disagrees with the local director of transport, the issue is referred to the director general of highways.

In some cases the regional director may consider that the submission 'should be seen by the secretaries of state', then the inspector's report is forwarded with the regional director's recommendation.

Above all the regional directors are told:

> The ministers should not be left to decide between conflicting official views without a firm recommendation if this can possibly be avoided. Where a conflict cannot be resolved . . . the case must be submitted through highways directorate and the chief planner.[32]

A lot of power is therefore concentrated in the hands of the seven regional directors. The best known of these was the one who was in charge of the south-east region from 1979 until his retirement in 1986. He was Joseph Peeler.

11 Business lunches

Just round the corner from the Department of Transport's office block in Westminster's Marsham Street is an expensive Italian restaurant called L'Amico. It is known in the department as 'the canteen' – so frequently does the FTA take civil servants there for lunch.[1]

The FTA is not alone in trying to buy influence through wining and dining. It is standard practice for all pressure groups. A lunchtime tour around the restaurants and wine bars that are the haunts of the civil servants from the Department of Transport will produce several clutches of lobbyists, civil servants and politicians. Not all the lobbyists are from the road lobby. But many of them are. And the road lobby can normally afford a better class of restaurant than the opposition can. When the SMMT was trying to fend off the campaign to remove lead from petrol, it held a series of lunches at Lockett's, one of London's more exclusive restaurants.[2] The FTA and the RHA regularly lunch with civil servants.[3]

The road lobby targets are the people with their hands on the levers of power, ministers, MPs, civil servants and officials in local government. These are the people who can arrange policies to suit the road lobby. And a friendly little chat over lunch is just one of the ways of getting at them.

The road lobby values its contacts highly. Some idea of the extent and scope of these contacts can be gleaned from the inaugural luncheon of the BACMI, in 1981. It was a chance to thank people who had helped the industry in the past, renew old friendships and cultivate new contacts. About 350 people sat down to the poached salmon, washed down with a pleasant Muscadet, at Grosvenor House, in London's Park Lane.

There were about 100 guests, including David Howell, the Secretary of State for Transport. Among the dozen or so MPs on the guest list was Peter Fry, the Conservative chairman of the All Party Roads Study Group. The deputy secretary at the Department of Transport in charge of roads lead a contingent of nearly thirty civil servants.

There were about forty county surveyors, and other senior council road engineers, as well as fifteen journalists.

The road lobby is known for its lavish hospitality. Certainly the BACMI's lunch was unremarkable by road lobby standards. When Margaret Thatcher, as leader of the opposition, spoke at the SMMT's annual banquet in 1975, there was an audience of 1,250.

Of all the influential people courted by the road lobby, the civil servants are the most useful. In terms of political investment they provide the biggest return for the least effort.

Civil servants conduct the administration of the government. They draft green papers, white papers and other policy documents. They draft legislation. They draft regulations, the secondary legislation, which is so important to road transport. And they advise ministers on policies, and their political consequences.

The civil servants are the minister's eyes and ears. The private office controls the flow of information reaching ministers. If they are sympathetic to the road lobby, they will ensure that the road lobby's case is well presented to ministers.

The information flows both ways. The value of friendly civil servants is not just to project the lobby's views into the department, but also as a source of information about what is going on inside it. Being in touch is vital if the lobby is to plan its campaigns successfully.

During the 1970s, the techniques of forecasting traffic became an important political issue. The traffic forecasts were one of the fundamental ways of justifying a road (we expect traffic to grow, therefore we need more roads). The forecasts came under attack from environmentalists, both at public inquiries and in the trade press.

The government responded, as it often does when faced with an unwelcome problem, by instituting an inquiry to dispense balm. As transport secretary Bill Rodgers put it: 'an independent view is greatly needed if the road programme is to be soundly based and to command respect.'[4]

The inquiry was headed by Sir George Leitch, a defence industry contractor, and was formally known as the advisory committee on trunk road assessment. The committee invited evidence from interested parties.

At the beginning of 1977, Transport 2000 asked for, and was given, an extra week to complete its evidence. The BRF was tipped off. It clearly suspected a machiavellian plot, and delayed the publication of its evidence for a week, so that Transport 2000 would not have a chance to counter its arguments.

The conspiracy was in the mind of the beholder, as it so often is.

Transport 2000 was then run by one person, part time. The evidence was late because the group was overburdened with work.

No inquiry is independent. Indeed the very description is normally reserved for those factions which agree with its conclusions. The Leitch committee, despite Rodgers' view, was no exception. The committee's composition was chosen to balance some of the conflicting interests, to try to convince both the road lobby and the environmentalists that the committee was going to be fair to them.

Two appointments, one from British Rail and the other from the Civic Trust, were designed to please the environmentalists. Three other appointments were people that the road lobby could scarcely object to.

Professor Peter Hall, of Reading University, was a long-standing supporter of converting railways into roads, and someone who believed that failing to build London's ringways was one of Britain's greatest planning disasters.[5] Tom Williams had built roads, before translating into academia, while the appointment of Bob Beckham was a direct result of pressure from the FTA.

Even so, when the committee's membership was first announced it brought immediate criticism from the road lobby. The senior vice-president of the Institution of Highway Engineers, who was Norfolk's county surveyor,[6] thought it 'significant that no one on the committee had ever planned or built a road'. This was rather unfair to Williams who was on the Institution's council. Another critic was unhappy at the absence of a BRF appointee.[7]

Leitch himself brought a distinctly quaint attitude to bear on his task. 'With weapons of war you judge by lethality. But how do you judge the value of a roads programme to the community?'

The Leitch committee's report, which was published in early 1978, did not favour the road lobby, and made a number of concessions to the environmentalists. One of the chief arguments for building roads was (and still is) that doing so would help economic growth, either nationally or in the regions. The committee concluded that this argument was 'weak and at best unproven'.[8]

The conclusion was, at least in part, a result of the composition of the committee. Most of the work was shared between the two youngest and brightest members. One came from British Rail and the other was an economist at the London School of Economics.

The conclusions upset both the road lobby and the Department of Transport, particularly since some of the report's more critical comments were widely reported. Sir Peter Baldwin moved swiftly to assure the department's staff that road building would go on:

there was no question about the continuing importance of highways as the recent Leitch report testified. This report [was] misrepresented in the press . . . Inevitably the departments would be more exposed to discussion with the public and he hoped that as a result public confidence in them would grow . . . over the last few years the departments had suffered from hurtful and misinformed criticism and this was particularly unfortunate in view of the sterling work of the staff.[9]

Ministers decided to make the committee a permanent fixture, renaming it the standing advisory committee on trunk road assessment. Three months before this committee was reconstituted, the BRF was knocking on the department's door, trying to ensure that the committee's composition was tilted more in its favour.

In March 1978 a BRF delegation, including its chief executive Robert Phillipson and its economist Shaun Leslie, went to the Department of Transport's headquarters. There, they met two of the most senior highways civil servants, Trevor Hughes, who had succeeded John Jukes as director general of highways (although the post lost this title), and John Lane, who was in charge of administering the roads programme.[10]

They discussed the Leitch report. The BRF was upset by the report's conclusions and wanted its own appointee on the committee. The civil servants did not hold out much hope. And the three new members of the committee did not include a BRF appointee, although one of the new members was a county surveyor, which could have been a nod in the BRF's direction.

Most of the contact between the road lobby and the civil service is informal, and secret. Indeed civil servants are under instructions not to reveal details of contacts with lobbies to parliamentary select committees: 'matters which are, or may become, the subject of sensitive negotiations with governments or other bodies . . .' should not be talked about.[11]

This secrecy is important to the success of the road lobby's contacts with the civil service. In pressure group politics, information is, if not power, then at least the prerequisite for it. If the road lobby is pursuing an issue with the civil service there is a fair chance that the environmentalists will not get to hear of it. (And before the environmental groups became better organised in the 1970s, this was a racing certainty.) Consequently the environmentalists would not be able to mount any effective challenge to the road lobby's initiative.

However, the power of the civil service is limited, mostly in administrative changes on matters which are unlikely to be politically controversial. (Although the extent of the controversy is clearly linked to the opposition's effectiveness.) And administrative changes, such as the one which effectively raised the maximum weight of heavy lorries from 38 to 40 tonnes, on the quiet, are exceptional. It is the sort of change that could only be kept secret in the tightly knit circle of the department's freight directorate.

Parliament is a much more open level of lobbying. It has the advantage that its power is virtually unlimited. Its disadvantage is that parliamentary moves are almost certain to attract the attentions of the opposition.

Information is just as important among parliamentary lobbyists. Charles Barker, a firm of parliamentary agents in the City, with a turnover of £1 million in the early 1980s, is retained by three groups in the road lobby, the BRF, the FTA and the SMMT. It provides these groups with a daily digest of events in Parliament, which affect roads, lorries or the motor industry. The firm is paid to monitor Parliament, so that its clients will not be caught napping. The firm is also a channel for planting parliamentary questions and feeding back the replies.

The road lobby's general parliamentary relations are conducted through the All Party Roads Study Group, which was founded in 1957, while the SMMT also has an All Party Motor Industry Group. The pattern of the roads group's events is fairly well-defined, with four or five meetings for MPs in the House of Commons, and a trip abroad.

The group meets in a committee room of the House of Commons, booked in advance by a friendly MP, and the meeting may be attended by up to a dozen MPs. The group has been less successful in attracting Lords to its meetings.

The talks are given by prominent road lobby figures. In 1977, for instance, David Plastow, the managing director of Rolls Royce, addressed the group on the subject of the 'motor vehicle in the economy'. He used the occasion to attack rail subsidies: 'Rail users are not bearing the full cost of the service they use.' Sharing the platform with him were the BRF's man Phillipson, and an economist from the SMMT, just in case there were any awkward questions.[12]

The highlight of the year, for the more assiduous attender, is the foreign trip. As Bill Rodgers put it, in his early days as a backbencher, the road lobby is 'generous in hospitality to members of parliament whom it takes to see road building achievements'.[13] In 1986 the MPs went to Canada.

These occasions provide the road lobby with an excuse to exercise the expense account, although this sometimes backfires. On a five-day jaunt to Chicago and New York in 1977, one MP went missing for the duration of the trip, only turning up to catch the plane home. And a fairly common resolve after each foreign trip is to try to ensure next year that the MPs are seriously interested in roads, and not just freeloaders.

The All Party Roads Study Group is the road lobby's background activity in Parliament. It helps to keep the case for roads in the forefront of MPs' minds, and enables the lobby to identify sympathetic (and hostile) MPs.

These MPs do not always cut an impressive figure in Parliament. John Horam said that the road lobby MPs are effective. 'Transport is a minority sport in Parliament. And they are always there, putting their point of view.'[14]

Parliament is one of the main channels for putting pressure on ministers and civil servants. If an informal approach to the civil service has been ineffective then the next stage for any well-organised pressure group is to enlist the help of a friendly MP. Sometimes the civil servants will even suggest this course of action as a way of giving them an excuse for taking up an issue.

Parliamentary tactics range, in rough order of effort and pressure, from written questions, to oral questions, through to a full-scale debate, or an investigation by a select committee. Each extra turn of the screw requires more effort, and produces more pressure.

Tabling a parliamentary question just requires the road lobby to contact a sympathetic MP, with a draft, which will normally be tabled unchanged. In 1984, the BRF alone tabled nearly 100 such questions.[15]

Inside the department, even the most innocuous written question has an immediate impact. A pink file with a red tab lands on a civil servant's desk. This question has to be given top priority. All other work must be dropped. Often a well-organised lobby will know the civil servant who will be thus troubled. The civil servant now not only has to prepare an answer to the question, but may also have to explain why the question is being raised and which pressure group has prompted it.

An oral question causes even more disruption in officialdom. The point of an oral question is that it will be followed by a supplementary question, the content of which is not broadcast in advance. The civil service has to anticipate all the likely supplementaries, and draft answers for them, so that the minister is not embarrassed. This necessarily involves a thorough knowledge of MPs' interests, and their links with pressure groups.

The next stage up the scale of pressure is to stage a debate. A full-scale debate will normally be staged by the government, or the opposition front bench. But there are a variety of mini debates which are more easily open to pressure groups.

The road lobby's tactics follow the precepts laid down by the BRF's long-term parliamentary adviser, Lt Commander Christopher Powell, more than thirty years ago.[16] Powell was one of the senior lobbyists. He celebrated fifty years in the business in 1978, during which he had been connected with the BRF for more than half of that time.[17] Powell laid down that pressure groups should be selective, but not too selective. They should study 'not only parliamentary procedure . . . but . . . the view point of individual MPs and what exactly it is they want in the way of information and data'.[18]

For the major debate on transport policy in 1977, the road lobby sent briefs to about forty MPs. Two MPs, Alan Fitch, the Labour chairman of the All Party Roads Study Group, and Hal Miller, now the Conservative chairman of the All Party Motor Industry Group, made speeches which reflected the BRF's brief.

The BRF again briefed MPs during the debates that followed the budget in 1977. The government wanted to increase petrol tax. The BRF, and the rural lobby, opposed this move.

Among the MPs who opposed the measure was Nicholas Ridley, who later became Secretary of State for Transport. Ridley has a notoriously poor grasp of detail. And many of the statistics he used in his speech also appear in the brief which the BRF circulated.[19]

The debate was a textbook manifestation of the lobby in action. In a confrontation with the government, a pressure group will try hardest to create dissent on the government's backbenches. (The opposition can usually be counted on to vote against the government.) In this case the Labour government was relying on Liberal support to stay in office. The combined weight of the road lobby and the rural interests persuaded the Liberals to oppose the tax increase, and the government was forced to withdraw it.

The road lobby also uses its parliamentary agents to organise visits for MPs in Britain, to see roads which it wants to promote. Frank Allaun, who was a backbench MP until 1979, recalled one occasion:

some years ago . . . the Lancashire group of Labour MPs, of which I was then the chairman, received an invitation to dinner to discuss the future of the county's roads, ostensibly from the Lancashire county council. However, while the LCC had doubtless concurred, the invitation came from a retired naval officer who was the chief PRO for the BRF, who were the real host and footing the bill.[20]

In the 1970s, a group of Yorkshire MPs was taken to look at the need for the M67, the motorway joining Manchester and Sheffield, which was to run through the Peak Park. 'Ostensibly it was a departmentally organised occasion. It turned out to be organised by the British Road Federation . . .'[21]

Although the opposition barely needs encouraging to vote against the government, opposition front benches are useful allies for any pressure group. Once out of office, a party no longer has any support from the civil service. Consequently, even front bench MPs rely extensively on lobbies for information, and briefing, about issues that can embarrass the government. And even if the front benchers refuse to deal with the road lobby directly, their party's research department certainly will have no compunction.

Albert Booth, who until 1983 was Labour's front bench spokesman on transport, had no sympathy with the road lobby's general aims. But he was keen to be briefed on the government's mismanagement of its road spending.[22]

The road lobby is, of course, only too eager to oblige. Sooner or later the shadow minister is likely to become the minister.

The road lobby was particularly close to the Tory party in the run-up to the 1979 general election. In 1977 a Conservative working party, headed by the shadow minister for transport, Norman Fowler, and including Peter Fry, produced a blueprint for transport.[23]

The new policy included several of the road lobby's most cherished aims, including slashing public transport subsidies and building new roads to 'aid economic recovery'. The policy called for the recognition of the importance of the car and 'the rights of the motorist . . . we reject deliberately anti-motorist policies'.

Fowler announced the new policy at the Conservative Party conference at Blackpool, and then went on to publicise it at an evening fringe meeting organised by the BRF's local group in the north-west.[24]

Of course being close to the opposition meant that the road lobby ran the risk of alienating the government. In a radio interview, Rodgers lashed out at the BRF:

> I think the British Road Federation talk a good deal of nonsense. I mean I find them a pretty irritating and rather irresponsible body of men. I wish they had a more constructive and helpful approach to some of these matters and didn't simply make press releases all the time. They're always welcome here to talk to me but I think they prefer this sort of confrontation approach to these matters.[25]

It was perhaps a little unkind to say that the BRF's approach was not constructive. But Norman Fowler sprang to the pressure group's defence: 'as that irresponsible body of men includes the National Bus Company and the National Freight Corporation I do find that rather extraordinary a description'.[26]

The last resort of any lobby, if it cannot persuade ministers, MPs and civil servants of its case, is a public campaign. The road lobby has only run a few public campaigns in the last forty years. Before starting one any lobby must stop, and think deeply about whether the issue really is worth pursuing that far. These campaigns are uncommon in British politics because they are difficult to conduct, time-consuming and expensive. They may also alienate people in power, whose goodwill may be sorely needed later. And finally, there is no guarantee of success.

In 1946 and 1947, the BRF and Aims of Industry, a right-wing pressure group, ran a public campaign against the government's plan to nationalise road haulage. All forms of transport had been coordinated by the government during the war as part of the war effort. The Labour government, which was elected in 1945, had been impressed by the efficiency of this wartime effort and did not want it lost with wasteful competition after the war.

Much of the campaign's propaganda was crude. One leaflet claimed 'nationalisation is going to put 60,000 hauliers – little men – who do a good job for you and harm no-one out of business'. Another said that queues at the shops would lengthen 'because deliveries . . . will be run by civil servants'.[27]

The campaign was designed to persuade MPs to throw out, or at least modify, the government's nationalisation measure, the 1947 Transport Bill. The campaign had little immediate effect, although the road lobby did forge close links with the Conservative Party, which persist even today. Certainly when the Conservatives regained power they denationalised road haulage.[28]

The same alliance and the road lobby and Aims of Industry came together again twenty years on, this time to try to defeat the 1967 Transport Bill. The Labour government wanted to ensure that heavy loads, being carried on long journeys (of more than 100 miles), went by rail wherever possible. Licences would be granted to road hauliers only if it was impossible to take the load by train. Newspaper advertising addressed to 'Mrs Britain' warned of dearer food. But again the immediate effect was minimal. The bill became the 1968 Transport Act, although the clause licensing lorries never came into effect, because the Tories won the 1970 general election.[29]

The road lobby, this time in the form of the Roads Campaign Council, again came together with Aims of Industry in 1955 to launch the 'roads crusade', the campaign for motorways. The verdict of George Strauss, a former junior transport minister, on this campaign was:

> the net effect of the pressure engendered in and outside Parliament by the Roads Campaign Council is to some extent responsible for the present increased expenditure on our road programme, inadequate though it is. Perhaps even more significant is that when the chancellor recently announced cuts in government capital expenditure, the road programme alone escaped the axe.[30]

If public campaigns are rare, the road lobby certainly does not neglect the press. All the main road lobby groups have at least one press officer, whose job it is to foster good relations with journalists. Selected journalists are taken to lunch. The FTA, for example, regularly holds lunches for small groups of journalists at the discreetly posh St Ermin's Hotel, near St James's Park.

The road lobby sets great store by its press coverage. Again, information is all. The BRF, for example, employs a press cuttings agency which monitors all the national press, regional and local papers as well as magazines. This agency clips all articles that include the key words selected by the BRF and sends these to it. The BRF has three key words, British Road Federation (not surprisingly), motorways and road – which must produce a fair haul of theological works.

A press report, or an item on radio or TV, is just another way of reaching the decision-makers. It signals to the people in power a degree of interest in an issue, and contains the implicit threat that public interest might increase to an embarrassing level. The civil service also monitors the press, and important articles may well be read by ministers.

Press coverage is a useful backcloth to a lobby's political activities. It helps to make politicians and bureaucrats more receptive, although public criticism can alienate those in power (as the BRF annoyed Rodgers). On at least two occasions, the ministry has blacklisted groups that were too strident.[31]

In its dealings with the press the road lobby has a built-in advantage over the opposition. This is the corps of motoring correspondents. These journalists' principal job is to test-drive cars. Their main interest, to judge from their articles, are topics such as the road holding of cars when cornering at high speed. They are a natural sink of sympathy for the road lobby. The heavyweight dailies often have a specialist transport correspondent on the staff.[32] Other papers tend to turn to the motoring correspondent to cover more general transport stories.

Ian Morton, the motoring correspondent of the *London Standard*, for example, frequently writes about road lobby campaigns, such as the BRF's demand for a tunnel under the Thames at Westminster, to bypass Parliament Square.[33]

12 Votes and wealth – the balance of pressure

The road lobby hijacked Britain's transport policy in the two decades following the end of the Second World War. It was the lobby's most consistently successful period, which made heavier lorries and motorway building almost unstoppable.

The key to this success was the virtual absence of any coordinated and effective opposition, which did not emerge until the 1970s, with the rise of the environmental movement.

Throughout its history, the road lobby has been at its most successful when the opposition has been weak, or non-existent.

Before the First World War, it faced no serious opposition. It achieved a Roads Board, with unparalleled power. Immediately after the war the Ministry of Transport was set up. Its main purpose was to build roads.

In the 1920s, the road lobby was divided. These divisions weakened it, and it was unable to keep the road fund intact. It united in the 1930s in the face, for the first time, of serious opposition, from the pedestrians and the railways.

The pedestrians forced through driving tests and a 30 mph speed limit in 1934. The railways forced the licensing of buses (1930) and lorries (1933).

After the Second World War, both these sources of opposition more or less disappeared. The road lobby was left on its own, and gained in power as the ministry became ever more complaisant. It was not that there was no public disquiet. There were protests about the increases in permitted lorry speeds and weights. And John Betjeman wrote to *The Times* about the M4 motorway spoiling the Berkshire Downs.[1]

But this opposition was fragmented and disorganised. It was like a first division football team playing a non-league side. The result was a foregone conclusion.

The balance of pressure did not shift decisively until about 1970. Suddenly the public found its voice. And the road lobby was rattled.

21 Part of the second 1,000 miles of motorway, under
construction at Swanley

22 One of the few checks on heavy lorries

It became increasingly strident as London's ringways were scrapped, motorway inquiries were disrupted and 40–tonne lorries were stalled. These are the tangible achievements of the environment lobby.

However, although the emergence of an organised opposition means that the road lobby has a stiffer fight, the balance between the opposing lobbies is still heavily weighted in the road lobby's favour. After all, the environment lobby has delayed 40–tonne lorries and many motorways. But it has not stopped them. And the Department of Transport has already started a softening up process, to prepare the way for ringway replacements.

Income is a rough and ready guide to the influence of a lobby, although it does not accurately gauge the voluntary effort that environmental groups depend on heavily. However, in a world where influence can be gained over lunch, a fat expense account can buy an awful lot of lunches – and at restaurants plush enough to flatter relatively poorly paid targets, such as civil servants, and MPs.

There are two important income thresholds for any lobby. The first is the point where a group's income is large enough for it to employ full-time staff. Beneath this income threshold a group must depend on volunteers.

Voluntary effort can make a big impact locally, as, for instance, in the case of the scheme for widening the Archway Road, in north London, where widening has been delayed for more than ten years. But voluntary effort alone is unlikely to have much impact on national policy.

For most people, the amount of spare time they have to devote to a cause, however passionately they believe in it, is limited, probably to a few evenings a week. It is difficult for a voluntary group to match the efforts of full-time lobbyists, who can nag away at an issue day after day. Whitehall works from nine to five, which is exactly when many volunteers have also to work for a living.

Thus, a group with an office and full-time staff has major advantages. The office will be a contact point for journalists, from Fleet Street, radio and television. They will ring up for information, a quote to bolster a story, or maybe just on the chance of stumbling across a story on a slow news day. Civil servants and politicians will also be able to contact the group when it suits them best, during the working day.

It was not until the 1970s that the environmental lobby had anyone working full time on transport. In the early 1970s, one person at the Council for the Protection of Rural England began to work part time on transport (and for the rest of his time on other countryside issues). At the Civic Trust, someone worked on heavy lorries. Transport 2000 started with one part-time staff member in 1972. It did not have full-time staff until the autumn of 1977. Friends of the Earth first employed someone to work full time on transport, the first such appointment in the environment lobby, in early 1975.

The second threshold is when a pressure group's income rises to the point where it can hire specialist staff, such as a lawyer, an economist or a parliamentary lobbyist.

The BRF and Transport 2000 are both broadly comparable groups. Both are alliances. Both play a coordinating role. Both are exclusively devoted to lobbying. And both groups spend a fair amount of their time opposing the other's initiatives.

In 1985, the BRF's turnover was about £340,000 – roughly nine times that of Transport 2000. This scale of income allows the BRF to employ, or retain, specialists including an economist who is responsible for the group's excellent statistics, and a press officer to build up good relations with the media. In 1985, the BRF employed fifteen staff. Transport 2000 employed three.[2]

The BRF employs a parliamentary lobbyist at an annual cost in the late 1970s of around £20,000. Transport 2000 depends on sympathetic MPs which it briefs prior to debates, and on the same MPs to tip off the group about developments in Parliament.

Of course the BRF does not have the advantages (or problems) of voluntary support. The BRF does not have individual members, and has relatively little involvement with the general public. There is little involvement of volunteers in the headquarters office of Transport 2000 (although this is not true of some groups in the environment lobby, notably Friends of the Earth). However, Transport 2000's network of local groups is run entirely by volunteers.

The BRF also has local groups. But as a local manifestation of support for the road lobby's cause (which is presumably their intention) they are risible. They are run by three full-time organisers. The energetic Jeremy Hawksley, who curiously is a Labour Party member, runs the London group. Gordon Lee, who is based in the Midlands, coordinates support for the road lobby among trade unionists in the motor industry, under the banner of the Campaign for the Defence of the Motor Vehicle. Maureen Orde, from a small office on the outskirts of Manchester, runs the BRF's activity in the rest of the country, from Hull to John O'Groats.

On most levels, the BRF's local groups are no match for Transport 2000's. Although the BRF's staff do have good contacts among key local officials, such as county surveyors.

One of the problems with voluntary support is that it can run out of control. A volunteer may prove to be disruptive, for example. It is not a problem that is easily solved. Volunteers cannot be sacked. Even the BRF has had its problems with local groups taking initiatives. In the 1970s it held a series of meetings at hotels to try and coordinate the activity of some of the more wayward groups.

The other drawback with involving the public is that it is time-consuming, which inevitably detracts from the effort staff can put into lobbying. At its most simple level, every group needs to raise money to keep going. The BRF, like most other groups in the road lobby, gets its money from a relatively small number of backers, writing large cheques. Most environmental groups (and in this case Transport 2000 is atypical) rely heavily on donations and subscriptions. Collecting a thousand £5 donations is much more demanding that handing over a cheque for £5,000.

The result of this balance of affluence is that the BRF works like a well-oiled machine. At Transport 2000, oil is one of the many things the group cannot afford. The research assistant to a shadow minister of transport recalls his first contact with the BRF: 'They knew what the game was about. The minute I was appointed they were in touch.' The researcher was taken out to lunch by the BRF's deputy director, at the Waldorf Hotel. 'They were trying to get their views across from the beginning. There was oodles of money.' At Transport 2000 the business lunch is more likely to be a pint in a pub, a cup of coffee, or a glass of wine.

The balance between the two groups is even more towards the road lobby than it appears at first sight, because of the two organisations' scope of activity. Transport 2000, in the mid–1980s, was monitoring the deregulation of bus services, promoting investment in railways, keeping an eye on the reform of traffic law as well as trying to restrain the road builders. Apart from its ritual public transport knocking, all the BRF's resources were concentrated on just one issue, building roads.

The final element in the balance of power between the two lobbies is the amount of pressure that they can bring to bear. A lot of the pressure is simply the result of good organisation, and the money that entails. But the government also has a dependence on the road lobby which the environmentalists can never match.

Many of the trade associations in the road lobby collect statistics for the government. And the government relies heavily on trade associations for information about their industries. Indeed one of the main stimuli for setting up trade associations was the First World War, when the government desperately needed a way of consulting industry, without having to talk to every small firm.[3]

The government still relies on trade associations. It even asked the

BRF to contact lorry firms in the 1950s as part of a survey prior to building the M1.[4] In 1973, when it launched an initiative to persuade the 100 largest firms to switch goods from road to rail, it turned to the FTA, which was a prudent choice if the initiative was intended to have no impact.

In the government's relations with trade associations, there is an implicit threat that they could withdraw this cooperation. The threat is of course more potent than the action. But even the AA and the RAC possess this power. In 1934, the government wanted to introduce driving tests. The AA and the RAC opposed tests. The government had wanted to use the motoring clubs as its testing agency. But the AA and the RAC refused to cooperate, thereby passing up a powerful weapon which they could have used later, in the hope of preventing the government from introducing tests. The government hired its own testers.[5]

People outside pressure groups often believe that arguments count, that the government comes to a rational decision after weighing up the merits of the opposing cases.

It is an understandable illusion. All pressure groups spend considerable time and effort gathering evidence to bolster their arguments. But what really counts is the power behind argument. It is a point that John Horam generally agreed with, although he said that his time as a minister was one of those rare periods when the content of the case counted.[6]

A former BRF employee made the same point, in a different way, when he observed: 'It was surprising how much influence the BRF had, given the weakness of its arguments.'[7]

The varying reasons for building roads are a good illustration that the argument matters far less than the power behind it.

In the 1960s, the need for new roads was obvious. The motorways would be faster. People would save time. This was self-evidently a good thing. So, at public inquiries in the 1960s, the ministry's engineers would justify building the new road on the grounds that it would remove a bottleneck.

In the 1970s, the engineers shifted their ground, in an attempt to cut away support from under the environmentalists. Suddenly the engineers said that the roads were designed to relieve towns of traffic. New motorways were suddenly styled bypasses – although the road had not changed one whit. The West Cross Route in London, for example, became the West London Relief Road.

Another of the arguments for building roads was that they would create economic growth, or new jobs. An official committee reviewed this argument in detail and dismissed it in 1978.[8] In 1980, the Department of Transport set out its road building objectives. The first aim was to build 'roads which aid economic recovery and development'.[9]

Another argument for road building is that it will speed exports to the ports (which ignores the fact they will also speed up imports). The BRF, for example, pushed its case for a dual carriageway A45 to link the Midlands with the east coast ports, under the banner 'the road to Europe'.

The argument has been propounded by ministry engineers at public inquiries since 1971, when Peter Walker, then Secretary of State for the Environment, said it was one of the major aims of his new enlarged road programme. In fact, as the National Ports Council's chairman pointed out in 1969 this was a very difficult argument to make stick. Trade goods spend only a small proportion of their transit time on British roads. Furthermore, trade traffic on a major route, such as the A45, was never more than a few percentage points of the total traffic.[10]

In London the arguments for road building have now been turned on their head. Originally when Bressey and Abercrombie proposed building a series of ringways, it was part of a strategy to move people out of the overcrowded metropolis. Today the Department of Transport and the road lobby argue for road building on the grounds that it will stop people leaving London.

A major reason for the road lobby's power is its allies inside the department, where the balance of pressure is just as heavily tilted in favour of the road lobby as it is outside. Although ministers do try to curb the power of the civil servants from time to time, they are unlikely to have any long-term effect. Ministers are transient. The civil service stays. The longest serving Transport Minister since the war lasted for six years. When Peter Lazarus retired as Permanent Secretary in 1986 he had been in the department for more than thirty years.

Ernest Marples, who was the second longest-serving Minister of Transport, had the most decisive ministerial effect on transport policy. But then he was pushing in the direction that the civil service wanted to go anyway.

The attempts by Barbara Castle and Bill Rodgers to curb the power of the road builders had some effect while they were in power. But once out of power the ministry reasserted its grasp on policy.

The most common case disputing the power to the road lobby is to argue that motorways and heavier lorries have been a product of some secular trend, or of economic growth.[11] Of course the growth in car sales, for example, has had an influence on government policy, if only because it has enriched the motor industry, and thereby the road lobby. But to take this argument to its logical conclusion is to say that governments are just passive slaves of economic forces outside their control. In which case it is difficult to see why such a feeble institution is so immune to pressure from the road lobby.

One of the clearest examples of government not just accommodating a tide of traffic is in Britain's major cities. In London, for example, there are many more cars than can possibly be used during peak periods. This is why the M25 filled up as soon as it was opened. There are too few roads for all the traffic, as there always must be while so many people in the capital own cars. Even if this is a result of pressure from environmentalists, it is still a policy.

There are two power bases for Britain's lobbies: votes and wealth. The road lobby's power comes from wealth. It is well-organised because it can afford to be.

The environment lobby's power comes from votes. It depends on the public to finance and to succour it. Of course the road lobby also has access to this source of power, but it has never been able to harness it, except arguably in the 1950s.

The different nature of these two power bases largely dictates the kind of pressure that the two lobbies can exert. Once roused, public opinion is immensely powerful and in the last analysis more powerful than the road lobby. But it is a blunt instrument. It is fine for stalling heavier lorries, at least for a while. But it is not easily amenable when a change in tactics is necessary. And public opinion tires, just as people do.

The road lobby's power is very flexible. It can change tack easily. Its power does not fade as time passes, so it can nag away at an issue for decades. And the road lobby is insatiable, as it has to be if its industries are to grow.

The road lobby is now laying its plans for the motorways of the 1990s, for new roads in London, and for heavier maximum lorry weights. The first step is to 40 tonnes,[12] then 44 tonnes, then. . . .

Appendix
The rival pressure groups

A short sketch of some of the groups mentioned in the text.

Aims (of Industry). A right wing pressure group set up to combat Labour's post war plans for nationalisation. The group helped the Road Haulage Association fight nationalisation in the late 1940s (unsuccessfully) and the Roads Campaign Council to launch its roads crusade in 1955.

All Party Motor Industry Group. Set up in 1981 by the SMMT to further its influence in parliament.

All Party Roads Study Group. Set up in 1957 by the Roads Campaign Council to press for more road building in parliament.

Asphalt and Coated Macadam Association. Set up in 1967 as a result of a merger of the Asphalt Roads Association and the Federation of Coated Macadam Industries. In 1981, as a result of another merger, it was replaced by BACMI.

Asphalt Roads Association. Became part of the Asphalt and Coated Macadam Association in 1967.

Automobile Association. See text for details.

Automobile Club. Founded in 1897, renamed the Royal Automobile Club in 1907.

Blue Route Action Group, one of the BRF's local groups, no longer active. It was based in Bradford.

British Aggregate Construction Materials Industries, was formed in 1982 as a result of a merger between the Asphalt and Coated Macadam Association and the British Quarrying and Slag Federation. Most of the major members of the Sand and Gravel Association and the British Ready Mix Concrete Association also joined the new group.

British Road Federation, see text.

British Road Tar Association, incorporated into the British Tar Industry Association in 1970. This latter association has now been dissolved.

British Transport Commission. The nationalised transport undertaking, which was set up in 1948 and dissolved in 1963, when British Rail was set up as a separate nationalised industry.

Bus and Coach Council. The trade association for bus and coach operators, which was set up in 1974, as the Confederation of British Road Passenger Transport.

Campaign for the Defence of the Motor Vehicle, a group set up by the BRF to foster support for road building among trade unionists in the motor industry.

Cement and Concrete Association. See text.

Civic Trust. An amenity group set up in 1957 to press for more conservationist policies in towns and cities. Became active in the campaign against heavy lorries 12 years later.

Commercial Motor Users' Association. The pre-war trade association for operators of buses, coaches and lorries. Set up by the RAC in 1905, as the Motor Van and Wagon Users' Association it was dissolved in 1945, the lorry operators splitting into two associations, the RHA and the Traders' Road Transport Association.

Conservation Society, set up in 1966. John Tyme's interest in motorways stemmed from his membership of the society's transport working party in the early 1970s.

Council for the Protection of Rural England. Founded in 1926, primarily because of concern about the growing impact of towns on the countryside. In the early 1970s it became active in supporting the Midlands Motorway Action Committee in the (unsuccessful) fight to stop the M40 and M42 being built.

County Surveyors Society, founded in 1885, see text.

Coventry Roads for Industry, a BRF group formed in 1985 to push for a north south road through Coventry.

Cyclists' Touring Club, set up in 1878, founded the RIA, but resigned in 1932 because of pro-motorist policies. Now a member of the opposition pressure group Transport 2000.

Federation of British Industries, now incorporated into the CBI.

Freight Transport Association, see text.

Friends of the Earth, founded in Britain in 1970. Became active in opposing roads schemes in 1975.

German Roads Delegation, see text.

Institution of Highway Engineers, founded in 1930 and now renamed the Institution of Highways and Transportation.

International Road Federation, founded in 1948, originally with offices in Paris and London. In 1964 it moved to Geneva. It also maintains a base in Washington.

International Road Transport Union, the international body linking bus and lorry operators.

London Amenity and Transport Association, the main group fighting road building, and lobbying for better public transport in London.

London Motorway Action Group was one of the leaders in the fight to thwart the ringway plans. It is now dormant.

London Roads Working Party, set up by the BRF in 1974, it became Movement for London.

M40 Roads Group, M40 Support Group and **M42 Support Group** were all off shoots of the Midlands Road Development Group.

Midlands Road Development Group, set up in 1973 by the BRF, not been active recently.

Motor Agents Association, the trade grouping for garages and the retailers of motor cars. The chief executive is David Gent, who formerly ran the BRF.

Motor Legislation Committee, set up in 1919 by the AA and the SMMT, its members included the Commercial Motor Users' Association and the RAC. It was wound up in 1943.

Movement for London, the BRF's London group.

National Road Transport Federation, set up in 1945 as an alliance of the RHA, the Traders Road Transport Association and the bus operators. It was wound up in 1963.

Northern Roads Group, a BRF local group which has not recently been active.

North West Roads Group, a BRF local group, founded in 1976, but has not recently been active.

Pedestrians' Association. Set up in 1929 and led the prewar fight for better road safety.

Permanent International Association of Road Congresses, set up in 1909 and reconstituted after the Second World War. See text for more details.

Road Haulage Association was set up in 1945, as a result of the break up of the Commercial Motor Users' Association. The RHA used the same name as a small prewar pressure group.

Roads Campaign Council, see text.

Roads Improvement Association, see text.

Royal Automobile Club, see text.

Royal Scottish Automobile Club, the Scottish counterpart of the RAC.

Society of Motor Manufacturers and Traders, see text.

South Western Organisation for Road Development (SWORD), a BRF local group, founded in 1976, which is no longer active.

South Yorkshire Transport Action Group, a BRF local group which was active in the 1970s.

Standing Joint Committee of the AA, the RAC and the Royal Scottish Automobile Club, founded in 1944 as a successor to the Motor Legislation Committee. The joint pressure group for the motoring organisations.

Standing Joint Committee of Mechanical Road Transport, founded in 1912 by Frank Pick, role subsequently taken over by the Commercial Motor Users' Association.

Surface Transport Action Group, the BRF's local group in Manchester. The group was still active in the mid 1980s.

Traders' Road Transport Association, set up in 1945 after the break up of the Commercial Motor Users' Association. It was the most important of the bodies which formed the FTA in 1969.

Transport Action Scotland was set up in 1974. It was still active in the mid 1980s. It spawned two sub-groups in 1975, the Edinburgh outer bypass campaign and the North East Scotland Access Group, neither has been active recently.

Transport 2000, founded in 1973 to fight for better public transport, and to encourage goods to switch from road to rail. Its members include the National Union of Railwaymen, the Civic Trust, the Conservation Society, the Council for the Protection of Rural England, the Cyclists' Touring Club, Friends of the Earth and British Rail.

Tyne and Wear Road Users' Group, a BRF local group which is no longer active.

West Midlands Roads to Prosperity, a BRF group which was set up in 1985.

Yorkshire and Humberside Road Users' Group, a BRF group which was founded in 1974. It is no longer active.

Yorkshire Roads Group, a BRF group launched in 1985.

Notes

1 Introduction

1 By 1987, according to the Department of Transport.
2 Department of Transport, *Transport Statistics Great Britain 1974–1984*, London, HMSO, 1985. All other figures in this chapter come from this source, unless otherwise specified.
3 Excluding public transport investment paid for out of fares.
4 Department of Transport, 1978/9 National Travel Survey.
5 *Ibid.*
6 Transport and Environment Studies, *The Company Car Factor*, London, London Amenity and Transport Association, 1984. The estimate includes all forms of company support for motoring.
7 264,000 Britons were killed in the war. By 1984 the total killed on the roads had reached 287,000.
8 Public transport travel dropped by 14 per cent in Britain between 1973 and 1983. The only country to have a sharper fall was Greece.
9 The sample this time is the twenty-four countries for which the Department of Transport publishes figures. Freight traffic is measured in tonne-kilometres.
10 Out of eighteen countries, only Sweden and Yugoslavia match Britain's record.
11 From 1962 to 1984. Figures from International Road Federation, *World Road Statistics*, Geneva, IRF, published annually.
12 United Nations, *Annual Bulletin of Transport Statistics for Europe*, New York, UN. The comparison is between 1963 and 1983.
13 BRF, The British Road Federation, BRF, 1968.
14 David Gent, a former director of the BRF, quoted in Mayer Hillman, *Personal Mobility and Transport Policy*, London, Political and Economic Planning, 1973, p. 109.
15 Figures for capital spending from 1971 to 1981 from Central Statistical Office, *Annual Abstract of Statistics*, London, HMSO, annual.
16 Department of Transport, press release, 8 November 1985.
17 BRF. *In roads*, spring 1978.
18 Geoffrey Potter, then director of the Asphalt and Coated Macadam Association, quoted in Transport 2000, *Transport Retort*, November 1979.
19 *New Statesman*, 23 November 1973.
20 Austen Albu, quoted in the BRF's 1960 annual report.

21 BBC radio broadcast, *World this Weekend*, Radio 4, 17 March 1985.
22 BBC radio broadcast, *Going Places*, Radio 4, 30 March 1979.
23 Interview with Albert Booth, July 1986.
24 House of Commons, *Parliamentary Debates*, 4 July 1973, Col. 556.
25 Arthur Bentley, 'The process of government, 1908', quoted in Geoffrey Alderman, *Pressure Groups and Government in Great Britain*, London, Longman, 1984, p. 269.
26 This information comes from Rob Edwards, a journalist in Edinburgh.
27 *New Scientist*, 24 July 1986.
28 This was said by the government consultants at the PTRC conference, University of Sussex, Falmer, 14 July 1986.
29 The Ministry of Transport's files on the nationalisation of Britain's main roads in 1936 are all missing.

2 Inside the road lobby

1 Des Wilson, *Pressure*, London, Heinemann, 1984, p. 7, makes a similar point: 'these organisations actually speak disparagingly of the undue influence of pressure groups'.
2 *The Times 1000 1985–6*, London, *The Times*, 1985. In order of turnover the companies are: Exxon (1), Shell Transport and Trading (2), General Motors (3), BP (6), Mobil (7) and Ford (8).
3 The power of the oil companies is described in Anthony Sampson, *The Seven Sisters*, London, Hodder and Stoughton, 1975.
4 *The Times, op. cit.*
5 William Plowden, *The Motor Car and Politics in Britain*, London, Pelican Books, 1973, p. 304, quotes this contemporary remark.
6 Pamphlets published by the BRF in 1946 carry this statement.
7 RHA Annual Report, 1972.
8 Hugh Barty-King, *The AA 1905–1980*, London, The AA, 1980, p. 238.
9 *Freight* (magazine of the FTA), December1981.
10 BRF Annual Report, 1985.
11 SMMT, *Annual Report 1985*, London, SMMT.
12 SMMT Annual Report, 1984.
13 *Guardian*, 21 June 1971.
14 Said by Charles E. Wilson to a Congressional Committee in 1952.
15 SMMT, *The Motor Manifesto*, London, SMMT, 1984.
16 SMMT Annual Report, 1984.
17 SMMT, *The Motor Manifesto, op. cit.*
18 Shell UK Ltd, *Annual Report 1985*, London, Shell UK Ltd, 1986.
19 They were the Asphalt and Coated Macadam Association, the British Quarrying and Slag Federation.
20 They are Blue Circle Industries PLC, RTZ Cement Ltd and The Rugby Portland Cement PLC.
21 1984 Annual Reports of the FTA and the RHA.
22 RAC's returns at Companies House (registered as the Automobile Proprietary Ltd) for 1979.
23 *Ibid.*, for 1974.
24 Barty-King, *op. cit.*, pp. 233, 243.
25 *Ibid.*
26 Plowden, *op. cit.*, p. 386.

27 Barty-King, *op. cit.*, p. 253.
28 *Ibid.*
29 *Ibid.*, p. 238.
30 RAC leaflet 'Close the Gap', London, 1981?
31 Minutes of AA's public affairs group, 11 October 1979.
32 Barty-King, *op. cit.*, p. 271.
33 *The Times*, 24 July 1975.
34 AA archives, public affairs group minutes, 11 October, 1979.
35 SMMT figures.
36 BRF letter to Jeremy Thorpe, 5 September 1974.
37 AA archives, Roads Campaign Council file, letter dated 7 October 1954.
38 *Ibid.*, 23 February 1955.
39 *Ibid.*, 10 March 1955.
40 *Manchester Guardian*, 11 March 1955.
41 Samuel Finer, 'Transport interests and the road lobby', *Political Quarterly*, 1958, 1.
42 AA archives, Roads Campaign Council file, *op. cit.* Circulation reached 102,000 in October 1962.
43 *Ibid.* The annual fee to the BRF was £3,500.
44 BRF Annual Report, 1963.
45 *Highway Times* (Roads Campaign Council's magazine), April 1961.
46 *Highway Times*, June 1961.
47 AA archives, Roads Campaign Council file, executive council minutes, 24 May 1961 and 28 June 1961.
48 *Daily Telegraph*, 3 October 1963.
49 BRF Annual Report, 1970.
50 British Industry Roads Campaign, *Roads for Prosperity*, London, BIRC, 1969.
51 BRF's company returns.
52 SMMT Annual Report, 1977.
53 SMMT's recommended BRF subscriptions in 1978 were that companies with a £250 million turnover should pay £5,000 to BRF; the other rates were on a crude sliding scale.
54 FTA Annual Reports.
55 Computed by the Labour Research Department.
56 Rees Jeffreys to Lord Stonehaven at Conservative Central Office, 1 November 1932, Rees Jeffreys' papers, in correspondence file.
57 *Transport Retort* (Transport 2000's magazine), May 1979.
58 Interview in *New Civil Engineer*, 27 October 1983.
59 Bill Francis, head of the institution's infrastructure planning group, *New Civil Engineer*, 1 May 1986.
60 International Road Federation, 'What is the International Road Federation?', leaflet, no date, but current in 1986.
61 Public Record Office.
62 PIARC Bulletin, September 1985, criticises *woonerven* (see page 91–3) and advocates 'less radical measures'.
63 Letter from William Rodgers, Secretary of State for Transport, to Frank Judd MP, 9 February 1977, quoted in John Tyme, *Motorways versus Democracy*, London, Macmillan, 1978, p. 79.
64 International Road Transport Union leaflet, Geneva, no date.

65 John Burby, *The Great American Motion Sickness*, Boston, Little, Brown and Company, 1971.
66 Bradford C. Snell, *American Ground Transport*, evidence to US Senate subcommittee on anti-trust and monopoly, S1167, Part 4A, Washington, US Government Printing Office.
67 *Ibid.*, General Motors' reply.

3   The growth of the road lobby

1   James Lightwood, *The Cyclists' Touring Club*, London, Cyclists' Touring Club, 1928, p. 225.
2   *Ibid.*, p. 226.
3   *Ibid.*
4   Cyclists' Touring Club archives, Box 4.
5   William Plowden, *The Motor Car and Politics in Britain*, London, Pelican Books, 1973, p. 14.
6   Lightwood, *op. cit.*, p. 233.
7   Obituary in *The Times*, 19 August 1954 and *Who was Who*.
8   *Ibid.*
9   William Rees Jeffreys, *The Kings' Highway*, London, Batchworth, 1949, p. 10.
10 Cyclists' Touring Club archives, *op. cit.*, Box 4.
11 RIA Annual Report, 1914/15.
12 *Ibid.*
13 Department of Transport, *Transport Statistics Great Britain 1974–84*, London, HMSO, 1985.
14 Rees Jeffreys, *op. cit.*, p. 12.
15 Allen Smith, *A History of the County Surveyors' Society*, Shrewsbury, The County Surveyors' Society, 1985, pp. 25–6.
16 Rees Jeffreys, *op. cit.*, p. 10.
17 Allen Smith, *op. cit.*, p. 26.
18 *Ibid.*, p. 27.
19 Rees Jeffreys, *op. cit.*, p. 18.
20 W. Ballin Hinde at the Paris Road Congress, 1908.
21 Rees Jeffreys, *op. cit.*, p. 78.
22 Recollections of an RIA member, *Cheltenham Chronicle*, 20 June 1959.
23 Plowden, *op. cit.*, p. 101.
24 Smith, *op. cit.*, p. 30.
25 *Ibid.*, p. 45.
26 Rees Jeffreys, p. 73.
27 K. Keir and B. Morgan, *Golden Milestones*, London, The AA, 1955, p. 47.
28 RIA Annual Reports, 1914–15 and 1916–17.
29 *Ibid.*
30 *Ibid.*
31 SMMT Annual Report, 1920.
32 Quoted in Philip Bagwell, *The Transport Revolution from 1770*, London, Batsford, 1974, p. 244.
33 Sir Gilmour Jenkins, *The Ministry of Transport and Civil Aviation*, London, George Allen and Unwin, 1959, p. 16.
34 Smith, *op. cit.*, p. 35.

35 Plowden, *op. cit.*, p. 212.
36 Edward Shrapnell-Smith, 'Five decades of commercial road transport', Henry Spurrier memorial lecture, 10 December 1945.
37 SMMT Annual Report, 1921.
38 Shrapnell-Smith, *op. cit.*
39 RIA annual report, 1928.
40 Plowden, *op. cit.*, p. 135.
41 Rees Jeffreys papers.
42 *Ibid.*
43 *King's Highway* (Asphalt Roads Association's magazine), 1928.
44 Plowden, *op. cit.*, p. 288.
45 RIA Annual Report, 1929.
46 RIA Annual Report, 1930.
47 *Ibid.*
48 RIA Annual Report, 1929.
49 Privileges and Rights Committee, minutes, July 1931, Cyclists' Touring Club.
50 Report to Cyclists' Touring Club General Purpose Committee, 18 March 1933, in Box 24.
51 *CTC Gazette*, June 1933.
52 RIA annual report, 1933.
53 Rees Jeffreys, *op. cit.*, p. 121.
54 Public Record Office, CAB 24/232.
55 Public Record Office, MT 33/130.
56 *Ibid.*
57 *Commercial Motor*, 29 March 1932.
58 Rees Jeffreys papers.
59 Rees Jeffreys, *op. cit.*, p. 269.
60 The Standing Joint Committee of Mechanical Road Transport Associations.
61 Public Record Office, MT 33/130, note taken by a civil servant.
62 Rees Jeffreys papers, file 21.
63 *Ibid.*
64 *Ibid.*
65 BRF's company returns.
66 Publice Record Office, MT 46/142.
67 letter to Rees Jeffreys.
68 AA Archives, RIA file.
69 Rees Jeffreys archives, file 21.
70 Sidney and Beatrice Webb, 'The story of the King's highway', quoted in Enid Wistrich, *The Politics of Transport*, London, Longman, 1983, p. 65.

4 One thousand miles of motorways

1 Rees Jeffreys papers, file 115, meeting on 2 July 1943.
2 *Ibid.*
3 Allen Smith, *A History of the County Surveyors' Society*, Shrewsbury, County Surveyors' Society, 1985, p. 26. William Rees Jeffreys, *The King's Highway*, London, Batchworth, 1949, p. 13.

4   William Plowden, *The Motor Car and Politics in Britain*, London, Pelican Books, 1973, p. 81–2.
5   BRF and SMMT, Annual Reports, 1935.
6   Smith, *op. cit.*, p. 44.
7   Rees Jeffreys papers, file 21.
8   BRF Annual Report, 1935.
9   John Killick.
10 Rees Jeffreys papers, file 39.
11 Rees Jeffreys papers, file 21.
12 RIA Annual Report, 1935.
13 Rees Jeffreys papers, file 39.
14 *Ibid.*
15 RIA Annual Report, 1935.
16 *The Times*, 6 November 1936.
17 *King's Highway* (magazine of the Asphalt Roads Association), July 1934.
18 Hugh Barty-King, *The AA 1905–1980*, London, Automobile Association, 1980, p. 172.
19 *Ibid.*
20 Public Record Office, MT 39/96.
21 *Ibid.*
22 *Ibid.* AA archives also have a report of the delegation.
23 *Ibid.*
24 *Ibid.*
25 *Ibid.*
26 *Ibid.*
27 *Ibid.*
28 *Ibid.*
29 AA archives, German Road Delegation file.
30 Public Record Office, MT 39/96.
31 *Ibid.*
32 BRF Annual Report, 1937.
33 AA archives.
34 Public Record Office, MT 39/508.
35 *Ibid.*
36 Rees Jeffreys papers, file 115.
37 *Ibid.*
38 Mervyn O'Gorman, *Road Transport and the National Plan*, London, British Road Federation, 1943(?), comments in Public Record Office, MT 39/508.
39 Rees Jeffreys papers, file 115.
40 *Ibid.*
41 *Ibid.*
42 Public Record Office, MT 39/509.
43 David Starkie, *The Motorway Age*, Oxford, Pergamon Press, 1982, p. 2.
44 Public Record Office, MT 39/519, and MT 39/657.
45 *Ibid.*
46 BRF Annual Report, 1948.
47 House of Commons, Parliamentary debates, 11 November 1948.
48 Public Record Office, MT 39/114.
49 BRF Annual Reports, 1948–51.

50 Public Record Office, MT 39/117.
51 *Ibid.*
52 *Ibid.*
53 *Ibid.*, contains a clipping (undated) from the *Daily Dispatch*.
54 *Ibid.*
55 *Ibid.*
56 *Ibid.*
57 *Ibid.*
58 *Ibid.*
59 *Ibid.*
60 *Ibid.*
61 James Drake, *Motorways*, London, Faber and Faber, 1969, p. 47.
62 John Boyd-Carpenter, *Way of Life*, London, Sidgwick and Jackson, 1980, p. 107.
63 Public Record Office, MT 39/117.
64 Roads Campaign Council leaflets.
65 J. F. Allan Baker, 'The general motorway plan', Institution of Civil Engineers proceedings, April 1960.
66 *The Times*, 23 and 29 January 1960.
67 *Ibid.*
68 *Ibid.*
69 House of Commons, *Parliamentary Debates*, 29–30 April 1963.
70 George Charlesworth, *A History of British Motorways*, London, Thomas Telford, 1984, p. 50.
71 Smith, *op. cit.*, p. 62.
72 *Ibid.*
73 E. Victor Morgan, *The Economic and Financial Aspects of Road Improvements*, London, Roads Campaign Council, 1965.
74 Smith, *op. cit.*, p. 64.
75 BRF Annual Report, 1971.
76 Richard Crossman, *Dairies of a Cabinet Minister*, Vol. 3, London, Hamish Hamilton and Jonathan Cape, 1977, p. 376.
77 Smith, *op. cit.*, p. 70.
78 AA archives have a note of this meeting, which took place on 22 April 1971.
79 Announcement made on 23 June 1971.

5 Bulldozing London

1 BRF, *Urban Motorways*, London, BRF, 1956, p. 218
2 BRF, *Summary of Activities 1958*, London, BRF.
3 BRF Annual Report, 1955.
4 BRF, *Urban Motorways*, *op. cit.*, p. 18.
5 Roads Campaign Council leaflets, 1955.
6 George Charlesworth, *A History of British Motorways*, London, Thomas Telford, 1984, p. 189.
7 David Starkie, *The Motorway Age*, Oxford, Pergamon Press, 1982, p. 31, quoting Sir Richard Clarke, *Public Expenditure Management and Control*, Macmillan, London, 1978, para 48.
8 John Wardroper, *Juggernaut*, London, Temple Smith, 1981, p. 29.
9 BRF, *People and Cities*, London, BRF, 1963, p. 11.

10 Starkie, *op. cit.*, p. 31.
11 Sir Colin Buchanan, *The State of Britain*, London, Faber and Faber, p. 59.
12 Wardroper, *op. cit.*, p. 30.
13 Colin Buchanan *et al.*, *Traffic in Towns*, London, HMSO, 1963.
14 *Ibid.*
15 BRF, *People and Cities*, *op. cit.*, p. 12.
16 *Ibid.*, p. 279.
17 BRF Annual Report, 1964.
18 BRF Annual Reports for 1964, 1965 and 1966.
19 Starkie, *op. cit.*, p. 39.
20 John Grant, *The Politics of Urban Transport Planning*, London, Earth Resources Research, 1977, p. 48.
21 London Regional Transport, *Annual Report*, 1985.
22 Mervyn O'Gorman, *Road Transport and the National Plan*, London, BRF, 1942.
23 Sir Charles Bressey and Sir Edwin Lutyens, *Highway Development Survey 1937*, London, HMSO, 1938.
24 Sir Patrick Abercrombie, *County of London Plan*, London, HMSO, 1943 (and *Greater London Plan*, London HMSO, 1944).
25 *Ibid.*
26 BRF, Annual Report, 1951.
27 Public Record Office, CAB 134/915.
28 BRF, *Urban Motorways*, *op. cit.*
29 F. A. Rayfield, 'The planning of ring roads', Proceedings of the Institution of Civil Engineers, Part 2, 1956, 5 pp. 99–135. Rayfield was the council's deputy chief engineer.
30 BRF Summary of Activities, 1958.
31 BRF Summary of Activities, 1960.
32 *Ibid.*
33 *Ibid.*
34 BRF Annual Report, 1960.
35 *Ibid.*
36 House of Commons, *Parliamentary Debates*, 26 October 1960.
37 Report dated 12 September 1966 by Director of Highways and Transportation, in GLC archives, file TD/GEN/1/69.
38 Letter from Robert Phillipson to Brian Martin, 27 February 1969, expressing concern about Hampstead, in GLC file TD/GEN/1/153.
39 In GLC file TD/GEN/1/232.
40 *Ibid.*, note from David Bayliss, dated 8 August 1969.
41 BRF comments on GLC's draft evidence, dated 21 May 1969, in TD/GEN/1/232.
42 In GLC's transport and development archives, File AD 15.
43 In GLC file TD/GEN/1/182 has notes of two meetings on 1 July 1968 and 20 February 1969.
44 Patrick Rivers, *The Politics of Pressure*, London, Harrap, 1974, p. 162.
45 Minutes of these meetings survive in GLC file TD/GEB/1/232.
46 *Ibid.*, letter from Williams to GLC dated 22 May 1969.
47 *Ibid.*
48 Michael Thomson, *Motorways in London*, London, Duckworth, 1969.

49 First leaked to the *Ecologist*, April 1973, letter (dated 10 October 1969) survives in GLC file TD/GEN/1/232.
50 GLC file TD/GEN/1/232.
51 GLC files TD/GEN/1/14.
52 Colin Buchanan and Partners, *The Conurbations*, London, BRF, 1969.
53 Colin Buchanan, *The Price of Posterity*, London, BRF, 1972(?).
54 BRF Annual Report, 1970.
55 Their case, largely compiled by Stephen Plowden and Michael Thomson, is inquiry submission E12/20.
56 ITN news broadcast, 9 August 1970.
57 GLC Transport and Development, file AD 45B.
58 John Nott to Desmond Plummer, 28 January 1969, in GLC file TD/GEN/1/153.
59 David Mitchell to Richard Brew, 9 October 1972, in GLC file TD/GEN/1/184.
60 Note from Vigars, 24 March 1971, in GLC file TD/GEN/1/16.
61 Richard Brew, quoted in *Daily Telegraph*, 7 May 1971.
62 AA public affairs group minutes of meeting held on 13 February 1975.
63 Report to BRF's public affairs committee, 22 February 1977.
64 Movement for London leaflets.
65 GLC, *Roads for London*, London, GLC, 1978, cut came in January 1981.
66 Standing Conference on London and the South East Regional Planning, *Routes for Longer Distance Traffic*, London, Standing Conference, 1980.
67 And still on the committee in 1984.
68 House of Commons Transport Committee, 'First Report from the Transport Committee (The Roads Programme)', Session 1980–1, HC 27–1, London, HMSO.
69 House of Commons, 'Government observations on first report of the transport committee', session 1982–3, HC 274, 1984. Minutes of evidence given on 15 February 1984.
70 Department of Transport, *Policy for Roads: England*, London, HMSO, 1983, Cmnd 9059.
71 Movement for London press release, 27 September 1983.
72 *New Statesman*, 20 January 1984.
73 *New Statesman*, 13 January 1984.
74 Department of Transport, *Reorganisation of Local Government in Greater London*, London, Department of Transport, 1983.
75 Department of Transport, Reallocation of Transport Responsibilities in London, London, Department of Transport, 1984.
76 Letter from Lynda Chalker to local residents dated 12 April 1984.
77 Speech by Lynda Chalker to the Battersea Conservative Association Supper Club on 17 September 1984. Conservative Central Office press release 601/84.
78 *Ibid*.
79 BRF/Movement for London, *To Keep London Moving*, London, BRF, 1983(?).
80 Department of Transport press release, 25 January 1985.
81 *Daily Telegraph*, 21 November 1984.
82 Letter from Lynda Chalker to William Shelton, dated 10 December 1985.

6 Motorway mania

1 John Tyme, *Motorways versus Democracy*, London, Macmillan, 1978, p. 28 has an account of the events. The farmer was John Burnhope.
2 Garry Turvey, of the FTA, speaking in Liverpool on 2 December 1970.
3 BRF Annual Report, 1973.
4 The number is imprecise because some groups had sub-groups.
5 BRF Annual Report, 1974.
6 *Transport Retort* (Transport 2000's magazine), June 1979.
7 Peter Kay, 'The British Road Federation's local groups', unpublished.
8 *Guardian* (a letter), 15 August 1978.
9 SWORD press release, embargoed for 19 May 1976.
10 *Transport Retort*, February 1979.
11 *Slough Observer*, 2 April 1976 and 9 April 1976. The original anti-M25 piece appeared on 12 March 1976.
12 *Guardian*, 11 August 1978.
13 Tyme, *op. cit.*, p. 54 and BRF's Public Affairs Committee meeting of 24 March 1977.
14 Tyme, *op. cit.*, p. 55; *Motorway Monthly* (later renamed *Transport Retort*) June 1977 and information from Peter Kay who attended the inquiry.
15 *Ibid.*
16 Speech by BRF chairman Tony de Boer, BRF press release, 13 June 1973.
17 *Ibid.*
18 Movement for London press release, 14 November 1978.
19 *Birmingham Post*, 24 May 1972.
20 Department of the Environment, *Transport Policy*, London, HMSO, 1976, p. 89, a passage written by Tony Crosland himself.
21 Speech to Institution of Highway Engineers, December 1976, see also interview in *Municipal Engineering*, 7 January 1977.
22 *Municipal Engineering*, 7 January 1977.
23 Headed by David Holmes and Frank Girling.
24 BRF, *Transport Policy in Britain*, London, BRF, 1976.
25 Interview with John Horam.
26 Department of the Environment, *op. cit.*, p. 69.
27 John Wardroper, *Juggernaut*, London, Temple Smith, 1981, p. 40.
28 Department of Transport, *Transport Policy*, London, HMSO, Cmnd 6836.
29 Council on Tribunals, *Review of Highway Inquiry Procedures*, London, HMSO, 1978, Cmnd 7133.
30 Sir George Leitch *et al.*, *Report of the Advisory Committee on Trunk Road Assessment*, London, HMSO, 1978.
31 Department of Transport, *Policy for Roads, England*, London, HMSO, 1978, Cmnd 7132.
32 Aire Valley Preservation Society press release, 10 March 1978.
33 Interview with Maureen Orde on Radio Pennine, March 1978.
34 BRF, *No Time to Stop*, London, BRF, 1979.
35 Allen Smith, *A History of the County Surveyors' Society*, Shrewsbury, County Surveyors' Society, 1985, p. 102.
36 *Inroads*, (BRF's magazine), October 1977.
37 Meeting took place on 3 February 1982.

38 Speech at Institution of Civil Engineers' Conference, 'Twenty years of British motorways', 1980.
39 House of Commons Transport Committee, 'The roads programme', session 1980–1, HC 27–1, London, HMSO, 1981.
40 Department of Transport press release, 17 April 1986, no. 198.
41 *New Civil Engineer*, 5 July 1984.
42 Department of Transport press release, 8 November 1985, no. 507.

7 Forty tonnes – what do you bet?

1 SMMT and Road Transport Organisations Joint Conference, held 29 December 1944, in Public Record Office, MT 34/189. They wanted 40 tons for a road train, and 30 tons for an articulated vehicle.
2 *Ibid.*
3 *Ibid.*
4 *Ibid.*, file suggests that the ministry was uncertain whether it should tell the committee.
5 *Ibid.*, Sir Alker Trip, of the police, was among those who were unhappy.
6 *Ibid.*, minute from N. Proctor-Gregg, 23 January 1947.
7 *Ibid.*
8 *Ibid.*
9 *Ibid.*
10 *Ibid.*
11 *Ibid.*
12 BRF Annual Report, 1950.
13 Richard Crossman, *The Backbench Diaries*, London, Hamish Hamilton and Jonathan Cape, 1981, p. 108.
14 MT 34/189, *op. cit.*
15 The Cabinet apparently thought Deakin's successor was called Arthur Cousins.
16 BRF Annual Report, 1957.
17 Public Record Office, MT 33/166.
18 *Ibid.*
19 *Ibid.*
20 BRF Annual Report, 1960.
21 Richard Kimber (ed.), *Campaigning for the Environment*, London, Routledge & Kegan Paul, 1974, p. 138.
22 The articles began on 21 September 1969; most were by Tony Dawe.
23 Article in *Motor Transport*, quoted in Kimber, *op. cit.*, p. 140.
24 Civic Trust, *Heavy Lorries*, London, Civic Trust, 1970.
25 Kimber, *op. cit.*, p. 150.
26 *Ibid.*
27 House of Commons, *Parliamentary Debates*, 29 November 1972, Cols 511–60.
28 *The Times*, 1 November 1973.
29 Foreword by John Peyton, *Report of the Lorries and the Environment Committee*, London, HMSO, 1973.
30 *Ibid.*; the membership of the committee was later widened to include more representatives from local government.
31 *Ibid.*

32 Department of the Environment, *Routes for Heavy Lorries*, London, DoE, 1974.
33 *Motorway Monthly* (later called *Transport Retort*), March 1977.
34 *Guardian*, 31 July 1978.
35 *Ibid.*
36 *The Times*, 5 October 1978.
37 Minute from Joe Peeler to Peter Lazarus, titled Lorry Weights, suggested inquiry, to Peter Lazarus, 16 October 1978.
38 *Guardian*, 30 October 1978.
39 *Freight* (journal of the FTA), January 1986.
40 Peeler, *op. cit.*
41 *Daily Mirror*, 1 November 1978.
42 *Daily Express*, 13 November 1978.
43 *Transport Retort* (Transport 2000's magazine), February 1979.
44 Sir Arthur Armitage *et al.*, *Lorries, People and the Environment*, London, HMSO, Cmnd 8439, 1981.
45 *Ibid.*
46 *New Statesman*, 2 January 1981.
47 FTA press release, 26 February 1981.
48 RHA press release, 2 April 1981.
49 House of Commons Transport Committee, *The Inquiry into Lorries, People and the Environment*, HC 192, London, HMSO, 1981.
50 Department of Transport press release, 1 December 1981, no. 359.
51 *Guardian*, 2 December 1981.
52 *Guardian*, 10 December 1981.
53 Department of Transport press release, 12 February 1986, no. 56.
54 Conservative Central Office press release, 16 February 1982, no. 123/82 and Department of Transport press release, 17 February 1982, no. 55.
55 Press release from CBI, FTA, RHA, SMMT and General Council of British Shipping, 8 March 1982.
56 CBI press release, 17 March 1982.
57 Department of Transport press release, 1 April 1982, no. 125 and 20 April 1982, no. 127.
58 Department of Transport press release, 28 April 1982, no. 138.
59 Department of Transport press release, 7 May 1982, no. 151.
60 Department of Transport press release, 14 May 1982, no. 156.
61 Department of Transport press release, 20 May 1982, no. 168.
62 *Financial Times*, 10 July 1982.
63 Conservative Party Conference press release, 8 October 1982, 650/82 and *Guardian*, 9 October 1982.
64 Department of Transport press release, 4 November 1982, no. 376.
65 Letter from Eastern Traffic Area of the Department of Transport, 17 August 1983, in *Transport Retort, op. cit.*, Vol. 8, No. 1, 1984.
66 *Ibid.*

8 Restraining traffic

1 *New Scientist*, 24 July 1986.
2 *New Scientist*.
3 Accident statistics for OECD countries, quoted in Mayer Hillman and

Stephen Plowden, *Danger on the Road*, London, Policy Studies Institute, 1984, p. 19.

4   *New Scientist*, 24 July 1986, and papers given at PTRC conference (L stream), University of Sussex, July 1986.

5   *Ibid.*

6   The official results of these experiments are contained in Sumner *et al.*, *Speed Control Humps*, Crowthorne, Transport and Road Research Laboratory, SR350, 1978 and LR1017, 1981.

7   Neither Friends of the Earth nor Transport 2000, for example.

8   AA archive. Meeting of Public Affairs group, 30 November 1978.

9   RAC statement quoted in national press, 26 August 1983.

10 *New Scientist*, 6 September, 1984.

11 *New Scientist*, 24 July 1986.

12 PTRC conference, *op. cit.*

13 BRF Annual Report, 1965.

14 AA statement quoted in national press, 5 September 1973.

15 AA and RAC press statements, quoted in national press, 22 March 1974.

16 AA press statement, quoted in national press, 15 December 1984.

17 Two adverts taken from the *Observer* colour magazine, 3 August 1986.

18 SMMT Annual Report, 1920.

19 Campaign for the Defence of the Motor Vehicle, and Midland Road Development Group statements, quoted in *Birmingham Post*, 10 October 1977.

20 Colin Buchanan, *Traffic in Towns*, London, HMSO, 1963 (report of the steering group).

21 House of Commons, *Parliamentary Debates*, 9 May 1977, Col. 983.

22 Transport 2000, *Nottingham Transport Policy*, London, Transport 2000, 1975.

23 The information comes from a visit I paid to Nottingham in 1974.

24 RAC Annual Report, 1975.

25 RAC press statement reported in national press, 14 January 1975; AA press statement report in national press, 1 May 1976.

26 RAC Annual Report, 1976.

27 *Ibid.*

28 AA press statement, reported in the national press, 16 February 1977.

29 Department of Transport press release, 16 May 1984, no. 231.

30 Department of Transport press release, 14 June 1984, no. 271.

31 *Transport Retort* (Transport 2000's magazine), December 1978, has a court report.

32 Derek Wood *et al.*, *Heavy Lorries in London*, London, GLC, 1983, p. 108.

33 CBI, FTA, London Chamber of Commerce and Industry, Movement for London, RHA and SMMT, 'London needs Lorries' report, 1983?

34 CBI press release, 21 July 1983.

35 'London needs Lorries', leaflet, published by CBI *et al.*

36 FTA press release, 2 September 1983.

37 GLC press release, 29 February 1984, no. 135.

38 Quoted in report on lorry ban to GLC transport committee, 12 December 1984.

39 Department of Transport press statement, 12 December 1984.

9 Buses, trains and the road lobby

1 BRF leaflet 'Backwards or forwards', 1938(?).
2 BRF leaflet, 'The railways and road competition', 1938.
3 House of Commons, *Parliamentary Debates*, 29 April 1963.
4 The report of the inquiry by Sir Ivan Stedeford has never been published.
5 British Railways Board (Richard Beeching), *The Reshaping of British Railways*, London, HMSO, 1963.
6 House of Commons, *Parliamentary Debates*, 29 April 1963.
7 *Ibid.*
8 *Ibid.*
9 Graham Wootton, *Pressure Politics in Contemporary Britain*, Boston, Lexington Books, 1979, p. 153.
10 *Ibid.*, p. 154, quoting advert in *The Times*, 10 April 1968.
11 Peter Walker, *Transport Policy*, London, Conservative Political Centre, 1968.
12 BRF Annual Report, 1967.
13 Barbara Castle, *The Castle Diaries 1964–70*, London, Weidenfeld and Nicholson, 1984, p. 372.
14 House of Commons, *Parliamentary Debates*, December 1967.
15 Wootton, *op. cit.*, p. 155.
16 Castle, *op. cit.*, p. 110.
17 British Railways Board, *European Railways Performance Comparison*, 1980.
18 Castle, *op. cit.*, p. 260.
19 *Sunday Times*, 8 October 1972.
20 Such as the North London Line Committee, see Kerry Hamilton and Stephen Potter, *Losing Track*, London, Routledge & Kegan Paul, 1985, p. 59.
21 The main national groups were the Railway Development Society, the Railway Invigoration Society and the National Council on Inland Transport. The first two have since merged.
22 Sid Weighell, then an assistant general secretary at the National Union of Railwaymen, was a prime mover.
23 *Building Design*, 30 March 1973.
24 According to the *Directory of British Associations*.
25 *Commercial Motor*, 19 April 1974.
26 Letter to Jeremy Thorpe, then Liberal leader, 5 September 1974.
27 BRF press release, 11 March 1976.
28 BRF, *Transport Policy in Britain*, London, BRF, 1976.
29 AA archives. Minutes of Roads Campaign Council Executive, 25 July 1962.
30 House of Commons, *Parliamentary Debates*, 9 May 1977, Col. 982.
31 *Inroads* (BRF's magazine), July 1979.
32 BRF and British Rail press release, 25 February 1981.
33 Department of Transport, *Railway Finances*, London, HMSO, 1983.
34 House of Commons, *Parliamentary Debates*, 3 February 1983, Col. 487.
35 BRF Annual Report, 1983.
36 House of Commons Transport Committee, 'The roads programme and the transport aspects of the 1982 public expenditure white paper', Session 1981–2, HC 334, London, HMSO, 1982.

37 BRF Annual Report, 1983.
38 Fourth Report from the Transport Committee, Session 1981–2, HC 334
    Evidence on 28 April 1982.

10 The partial ministry

1   Joe Peeler, 'Lorry Weights', a minute to Peter Lazarus, 13 October 1978.
2   *Ibid.*
3   *Guardian*, 30 October 1978.
4   Peeler, *op. cit.*
5   Barbara Castle, *The Castle Diaries, 1964–70*, London, Weidenfeld and
    Nicholson, 1984, p. 265.
6   *Ibid.*, and the *Guardian*, 6 January 1966.
7   RAC, 'Protecting the interests of the motorist', report of RAC public
    policy committee, London, RAC, varying dates.
8   Interview with John Horam, August 1986.
9   *Ibid.*
10 Interview with a civil servant, 1986.
11 Interview with Roger Liddle, July 1986.
12 Sir Gilmour Jenkins, *The Ministry of Transport and Civil Aviation*,
    London, George Allen and Unwin, 1959. pp. 34–5.
13 *Ibid.*
14 They persuaded the minister to set up the Salter inquiry, for example.
15 Written answer by Nicholas Ridley, to question from Bob Hughes, 11
    February 1986.
16 Advisory Committee on Trunk Road Assessment, *Report*, London,
    HMSO, 1977.
17 Jeremy Richardson, *Governing under Pressure*, London, Martin
    Robertson, 1979.
18 Maybury chaired the RAC's transport committee in the early 1930s.
    Killick was vice-chairman of the RIA until his death in 1952.
19 The other two are E. B. Hart and George Wilson, both of whom went
    to work for the Asphalt Roads Association during the 1940s.
20 RAC Annual Report, 1975, contains an obituary of Glanville.
21 The county surveyor is John Wilkes of Somerset. Quoted in BRF, *Urban
    Motorways*, London, BRF, 1956, p. 36.
22 He was also active in the AA. He died in 1984.
23 And was on the RAC's public policy committee until 1981.
24 Paper given at University of Southampton conference on Transportation
    and Environment, 1973.
25 *New Civil Engineer*, 1 May 1986.
26 Public Record Office.
27 Public Record Office.
28 Public Record Office.
29 Public Record Office.
30 John Adams, *Transport Planning*, London, Routledge & Kegan Paul,
    1981, p. 185.
31 Hugh Gardner (inspector), 'Report on public inquiry into Water Orton
    section of M42', Department of Transport, 1978.
32 Paper presented by Mark Sullivan to Cities Before Roads conference
    (organised by Transport 2000), 1986.

11 Business lunches

1 Brass Tacks programme, *Heavier Metal*, Manchester, BBC TV, 1984.
2 Des Wilson, *Pressure*, London, Heinemann, 1984, p. 7.
3 John Wardroper, *Juggernaut*, London, Temple Smith, 1981, p. 21.
4 Quoted in *Motorway Monthly* (now *Transport Retort*), March 1977.
5 Peter Hall in *The Times*, 9 April 1980.
6 *Motorway Monthly, op. cit.*
7 *The Times*, 31 January 1977.
8 Advisory Committee on Trunk Road Assessment, *Report*, London, HMSO, 1977.
9 Minutes of Whitley council meeting, 25 January 1978, quoted in *Transport Retort*, June 1978.
10 Held on 6 March 1978.
11 Civil Service Department, Memorandum of guidance for officials appearing before select committees, 1980, quoted in Geoffrey Alderman, *Pressure Groups and Government in Great Britain*, London, Longman, 1984, p. 78.
12 From copy of speech handed out at the meeting.
13 William Rodgers, *What shall we do with the Roads?* Fabian Society, 1959.
14 Interview with John Horam, August 1986.
15 BRF Annual Report, 1984.
16 Lt Commander Christopher Powell, 'Public relations and Parliament', Institute of Public Relations Journal, 27 September 1955.
17 Jim Callaghan, the prime minister, made a presentation to Powell.
18 Powell, *op. cit.*
19 BRF brief for Finance Bill debate, 5 May 1977.
20 Frank Allaun, letter to *New Statesman*, 23 November 1973.
21 Quoted in John Tyme, *Motorways and Democracy*, London, Macmillan, 1978, p. 70.
22 Interview with Albert Booth, July 1986.
23 Norman Fowler *et al.*, *The Right Track*, Conservative Political Centre, 1977.
24 *Inroads* (BRF's magazine), October 1977.
25 *Going Places*, interviews, BBC, Radio 4, March 1979.
26 *Ibid.*
27 Leaflets published by BRF and RHA in 1946–7.
28 An account of this appears in Samuel Finer, *Anonymous Empire*, London, Pall Mall, 1958, p. 68.
29 An account of this appears in Graham Woolton, *Pressure Politics in Contemporary Britain*, Boston, Lexington Books, 1979, p. 154.
30 George Strauss, 'Pressure groups I have known', *Political Quarterly*, 1958, 1.
31 Friends of the Earth in the early 1970s and Associated Road Operators (head Roger Sewill) in the 1930s.
32 In mid 1986 the *Daily Telegraph*, the *Financial Times* and *The Times* all had transport correspondents. The *Guardian* after employing a transport correspondent for many years had lacked one for several months. The *Independent's* policy was not clear as the book went to press.
33 *London Standard*, 13 May 1985.

12 Votes and wealth – the balance of pressure

1   *The Times*, 27 April 1962, quoted in Richard Kimber and Jeremy Richardson, *Campaigning for the Environment*, London, Routledge & Kegan Paul, 1974, p.110.
2   Company returns, and information from these groups.
3   Lord Devlin, *Report of the Commission of Inquiry into Industrial and Commercial Representation*, London, CBI, 1972.
4   BRF Annual Report, 1955.
5   William Plowden, *The Motor Car and Politics in Great Britain*, London, Pelican Books, 1973, p. 287.
6   Interview with John Horam, August 1986.
7   Interview with former BRF employee, March 1986.
8   The Advisory Committee on Trunk Road Assessment, Report, London, HMSO, 1977.
9   Department of Transport, *Policy for Road: England, 1981*, London, HMSO, 1982, Cmnd 8496.
10 Alisdair Aird, *The Automotive Nightmare*, London, Hutchinson, 1972, p. 85.
11 David Starkie, *The Motorway Age*, Oxford, Pergamon Press, 1982, p. 115.
12 Reg Dawson, a former civil servant in the department's freight directorate, advised the road lobby to 'lie low' with its campaign for 40–tonners in the run up to the general election. *Freight* (FTA's magazine) August 1986.

Index